FIRMLY P
an imprint of

~Living~
Through Crises

B. Dale Taliaferro

LIVING THROUGH CRISES
published by Firmly Planted Publications
an imprint of Equipped for Life Ministries

Copyright © 2003, 2005 by B. Dale Taliaferro
International Standard Book Number: 978-0-9764305-0-6

Printed in the United States of America

Scripture quotations taken from the New American Standard Bible®, Copyright © 1960, 1962, 1963, 1968, 1971, 1972, 1973, 1975, 1977, 1995 by The Lockman Foundation (www.Lockman.org). Used by permission.

ALL RIGHTS RESERVED
No part of this publication may be reproduced, stored in a retrieval system, or transmitted, in any form or by any means, without prior written permission.

For information:
Equipped for Life Ministries
P.O. Box 12013
Dallas, Texas 75225
U.S.A.
www.e-l-m.org

Library of Congress Control Number: 2005902339

Printed in the United States by Morris Publishing
3212 East Highway 30
Kearney, NE 68847
1-800-650-7888

First Edition | Fourth Printing | May 2012

*With special thanks to Carol, Ryan, and the
many friends who prayed*

*And with a heart humble and grateful for
God's grace in allowing me to glimpse a
portion of who He is and what He has
provided for His children, as we place our
trust wholly and confidently in Him,
finding Him our All in All*

PRINCIPLE ONE
Our most pressing need is not more time to work through our trials; our most pressing need is a new life to handle our trials!

PRINCIPLE TWO
God will lead us into trials, situations that we do not want to experience, in order to sensitize us to our continuing, natural resistance to His will and to uncover our false pride.

PRINCIPLE THREE
God may send us into situations in which we feel estranged from Him, when in fact, He is ever watching over us.

PRINCIPLE FOUR
God will repeat His tests so that we can learn His lessons from them.

PRINCIPLE FIVE
Being weary physically and frightened emotionally may hinder our spiritual responsiveness.

PRINCIPLE SIX
Because of our sinfulness, we will be frightened even at the solution that God sends for our troubles.

PRINCIPLE SEVEN
Our present reliance on Jesus always will manifest itself in present obedience.

PRINCIPLE EIGHT
When we respond to God in the midst of our trials, regardless of the severity of our emotional state, we can begin to have immediate spiritual victory.

PRINCIPLE NINE
The same fears and distresses which paralyzed us once will return if we take our eyes off Jesus.

PRINCIPLE TEN
If we do not respond properly to the trial facing us now, we may not be ready for the next trial, which is already on its way toward us.

Table of Contents

Preface   7

Introduction   11

Background to Our Passage   21

~Living~ Through Crises

    PRINCIPLE ONE   43
    PRINCIPLE TWO   52
    PRINCIPLE THREE   58
    PRINCIPLE FOUR   63
    PRINCIPLE FIVE   68
    PRINCIPLE SIX   72
    PRINCIPLE SEVEN   84
    PRINCIPLE EIGHT   90
    PRINCIPLE NINE   100
    PRINCIPLE TEN   109

Preface

Two brief explanations will be helpful to readers of this book. First, in coming chapters, "deliverance" refers to a spiritual deliverance. God certainly has the capacity to remove our trials or remove us from them. But He may also sustain us by His grace as we endure our trials. It is to this sustaining grace that I refer when I use the word "deliverance." With this grace, God removes our fears, quiets our hearts, sustains our perseverance, engenders our joy, and supplies to us every provision that we need to endure our trials with a sweet contentment accompanied with great expectation.

Secondly, the reader needs to be familiar with two passages in the Bible. They are found in Matthew's gospel, chapter 10:1-15 and chapter 14:13-33. I advise the reader to examine these passages over and over again, until the events that transpired in them can be recalled readily. Familiarity with these texts will greatly help the reader grasp the principles that I will draw from them.

It is my deepest wish and prayer that this little book will be of help to you as you face the trial that God has brought into your life. And I would greatly like to hear from you if it is. Please do not hesitate to contact me through the publisher. May God bless you.

Introduction

As I pick up the pen to write this introduction, I am waiting for the phone to ring. I am expecting a call from my doctor. After he examines my CAT scans, he is going to diagnose a certain ominous "spot" on my right kidney.

About nine years ago, I had surgery to remove a cancerous tumor in my left kidney. Actually, my whole left kidney was removed as a precautionary step, since the cancer was quite large and of a very deadly sort, a renal cell carcinoma. I would like to tell you about that experience in order to glorify our Lord and in order to illustrate the provisions that He offers as we navigate the trials that He sets before us.

"Mr. Taliaferro, you have a mass on your left kidney," the radiologist informed me after examining my sonogram. He gave out his news without emotion, as though he were reading a weather report for a city somewhere in the world that he had no interest in or desire to see. I am sure his intent was to try not to alarm me any further than his plain declaration would by itself. "Your surgeon will explain what this means and what needs to be done," he said just before leaving the room.

This was not what I expected to hear ten years ago in August of 1993. My thoughts spiraled downward as I returned to the urologist's office. A short time later (though it seemed like an eternity) I was informed by my doctor that I had a malignant tumor on my kidney and that it needed to be removed as soon as possible.

Cancer? Me? Surely not—it has always been someone else. But the telltale signs of blood in my urine and the excruciating back pain told me that all was not well, even though everything else about me indicated that I was healthy. As I pondered my situation, things looked grim (I will not go into detail about the despairing thoughts that seemed to come into my mind from every direction). But I am thankful that my state of mind and my emotions soon changed! After despairing for fifteen or twenty minutes, I said to myself, "This is insane! My God has not changed! He is the same at this very minute that He was yesterday and the day before and the year before that." I began to consider His glorious character and how He had demonstrated His faithfulness and His love and protection toward my family and me over the past twenty-three years, and in minutes my heart was flooded with the most wonderful peace and joy one could ever imagine. My God had begun to do "exceedingly, abundantly beyond what I could ask or think."[1]

My only concern as I headed home was how Waunee, my wife of twenty-four years, and Ryan and Shannon, our children, would respond to the news that I had to bring them. I did not know that our dear doctor and friend had already called and shared the situation with them, or that they had been sitting on the sofa, hand-in-hand, praying for me. When I arrived home, we came together and prayed, giving thanks to God for being the same that moment as He always had been for all the years we had known Him. We thanked Him for the situation and asked only that He would enable us to respond in such a way that He would receive glory from our lives throughout the trial. We knew that it would be short in comparison to eternity and light in comparison to the eternal weight of glory that He would give to us out of His abundant mercy and grace.[2]

That night we spent a relaxing evening together. I did not realize how hard Waunee was struggling to hold back her tears. She quietly called a few of our close friends to pray. This set in motion the most amazing amount of prayer on our behalf that we had ever known. We could never have imagined the scores of believers who would intercede on our behalf. It seemed as if the

---

[1] Ephesians 3:20.
[2] 2 Corinthians 4:16-18.

entire country, and beyond, was praying for us. We heard for months and months after the surgery about the churches, prayer chains and Bible studies that were bringing us continually before the throne of grace.[3] As believers prayed, God answered those prayers and filled us with such grace that it was clear that our response was supernatural to all who were observing it. It was not something we could have conjured up. Our peace was truly one which "surpassed all comprehension." By noon the next day, Waunee began to realize that God was doing a mighty work in our lives. We had no idea what the outcome would be, but we did know that it would be "good" and that God would glorify Himself in it. With these ends we were fully content.

The surgery, which was supposed to take place as soon as possible, was delayed for eight days. When we first heard of the delay, it seemed not only pointless but dangerous to us. But we did not begin to worry; we knew God was in control and that He must have special plans for us in the intervening days. We were right in our expectations, for we had wonderful opportunities to share with groups and individuals what God was doing in our lives and how He was proving Himself faithful to us.[4] I saw God do more in those few days in some individuals' lives than I was able to accomplish in ten years of ministering to them. God's presence, power and compassion were so evident at this time that everyone watching us understood that God's grace clearly was sustaining us in every imaginable way. These were very special times! Even though we did not have any idea to what conclusion God would bring our trial, our peace and joy and our confidence, reliance and steadfastness in the Lord grew daily.

But then we discovered another reason for the delay. A precious friend went to be with the Lord, and we were able to

---

[3] Hebrews 4:14-16.
[4] Psalm 119:75.

spend some time with her sister, another special friend. How glad we were that we were not in the hospital but were available to encourage and console this dear friend. Our Lord's timing is always perfect in all that He does!

The days we waited were extraordinary. While we went about our lives in a somewhat normal fashion, our times together as a family were especially precious. We had a "game night" with friends, laughing in a wonderful time of fellowship together. We even slept peacefully each night. This was a major miracle for Waunee who has always been a very light sleeper.

When the day for the surgery arrived, the hospital did not seem strange at all. It felt normal: we knew that this was the place we were supposed to be! There were four of us in the room when the nurse came in. Ordinarily, patients about to undergo major surgery are readily identifiable by their melancholy demeanor, but she had to ask which one of us was really Mr. Taliaferro. You would not have believed how fast the other three men came out of the room at that point!

A second-year resident who was going to be in the operating room (with four other doctors) came in to talk to me about the operation. I was so cheerful, she apparently decided that I did not know or understand the severity of my situation. Finally she tactfully asked what the doctors had told me about my impending surgery. I looked at her and said, "I have a malignant tumor on my left kidney and you are going to cut the cancer out or, if need be, remove my whole kidney." As we talked further I made sure she knew that I understood that my situation was a serious one. I knew that if the cancer had metastasized, it would be only a matter of time. At this point she put down her clipboard and asked, "What exactly do you do?" She was impressed with my sense of peace and joy. What an opportunity I had to share the wonderful sufficiency of my Lord and Savior!

Waunee and I agreed together that her role during the operation was to pray. The evening before I went to the hospital, she and I picked out the passages in the Bible that we thought would be most meaningful to those who might come to pray in my hospital room. We wanted everyone to focus on the Lord and "praise Him for His mighty deeds and [praise Him also] according to His excellent greatness."[5] Focusing upon the "problem" in times like these never helps one to respond as one should. We wanted to fix everyone's eyes on Jesus; He, and He alone, is the solution to life's every problem.

We placed a note on the door to let visitors know that my room would be a place of prayer and praise during the surgery and that everyone was welcome to come in to pray and to praise God. The note also mentioned that others would be keeping watch in the nearby waiting rooms. The room was filled all day. We later learned that so many people stopped at the information desk that the volunteer eventually knew my room number by heart! Another friend told us that when she asked about me, she was told, "Some are in the second floor waiting area, some are in the twelfth floor waiting area and some are in his room. They seem to be everywhere!" God is so good! He provides the power as well as the encouragement we need in times of trials.

Some very special friends drove back from their family vacation to be with us that day. The wife, a noted and gifted Bible teacher for over twenty-five years, read and explained the Bible passages that we had chosen (plus added some others). She and I are very like-minded, and Waunee said that it was as if I had been sitting in the chair beside her, instead of our friend, because her words and thoughts so closely reflected my own.

When my surgery was completed, just as the group in my room was singing "The Joy of the Lord is My Strength," one of

---

[5] Psalm 150:2.

my doctors opened the door, beaming. He was soon joined by another surgeon, and together they explained that they felt that the operation could not have gone better! There was much rejoicing in that hospital that night! In fact, Waunee was afraid that everyone was going to be asked to leave, including her, because the group became so noisy.

We still had to wait almost three days for the pathologist's report. I kept calling it the autopsy report by mistake. Waunee kept saying to me, "No, that one is not coming for awhile!" Our peace and joy continued uninterrupted over those three days because "our minds were set on the Lord."[6]

During that first night my pain was very intense, and it took about seven hours to bring it under control. Over and over again, I would say to Waunee, "Pray for me." She said each time she began to pray aloud, within seconds my body would relax and my face would be at peace. About the third time this happened she began to cry. She said it was so obvious that God knew my need before she even asked. It was clear, she said, that He was going before us each step of the way. What a simple truth: "We have not because we ask not."[7] Why would we ignore such a promise so consistently? Waunee prayed that night, "Lord, please help me to always remember this truth."

Over and over we saw God answer specific prayers in the hours and days that followed. My progress was rapid; by noon the day after the surgery, I was walking the halls. After that we walked them over and over and over. At one o'clock in the morning the following day, the nurses offered me a sleeping pill when they saw Waunee and me again walking the halls!

The long awaited pathologist's report finally came—ALL CLEAR! There was no trace of cancer anywhere else! The tumor

---

[6] Isaiah 26:3.
[7] James 4:2.

had come within three millimeters of penetrating the kidney sack, but had not yet done so! We were thrilled! They said that they anticipated that we would be in the hospital for at least another week so that the urologist, who was in charge of the surgery, could check up on me when he came back from his vacation. When he returned, he was amazed that I had been released from the hospital after only five days!

The day we were getting ready to leave the hospital, a nurse came down to the room. She told us that she was a Christian, and then said, "This is a cancer floor. The people who come here are very sad, anxious and fearful, even though many of them are Christians. But you and your family have been so different. There has been nothing about your countenances that has said, 'CANCER!' There has been nothing on your faces but joy the entire time you have been here, even while you were waiting for the pathologist's report. You are the talk of this floor—you have no idea what an impact you have made!" We tried to explain the simple truths that you are about to read in this book: "It is no longer I who lives, but Christ who lives in me."[8] All of our adequacy comes from the Lord.[9] God had been faithful to give to us what He had promised to give, in order to sustain us in our struggles.

Our prayers had been answered. God had poured out His mercy on us, and He had been honored and glorified! Our hearts had overflowed with joy throughout our trial. He had proven faithful to His promise to be our All in All. We had experienced the "normal Christian life," as Watchman Nee liked to call it.[10]

How we want this for you! It is available to all believers alike, every moment of every day, regardless of the severity of

---

[8] Galatians 2:20.
[9] 2 Corinthians 3:5-6.
[10] This is the title of one of his books on the Christian life.

the situation that you are experiencing. I believe that part of the reason our Lord allowed this trial to enter my life was to demonstrate that no trial need be overwhelming. Since "there is no good thing that dwells within any of us,"[11] we must conclude that "apart from Jesus, we can do nothing."[12] But *through Him* we already have been made "more than conquerors"[13] (i.e., super-conquerors!). And since we are conquerors, we ought to expect to conquer our trials and not be overcome by them!

That is what this book is written to help you do: become super-conquerors. May God become the Deliverer to you that He has been to me. As I wait for my doctor's phone call about the spot on my other kidney, I will be trusting Jesus to provide for me the same spiritual victory that He gave me ten years ago. Once again I have no idea to what conclusion God desires to bring my health problem. But that is not my concern—because it is not my problem! My only concern is that I trust Jesus throughout my trial so that He receives all the glory. If He is glorified, I know I will be pleasing in His sight. And if I am pleasing in His sight, I know He will once again provide "exceedingly, abundantly beyond all that I could ask or think." What an adventure!

---

[11] Romans 7:18.
[12] John 15:5.
[13] Romans 8:37.

Background to Our Passage
MATTHEW 10:1-15 & MATTHEW 14:13-21

This book studies the famous Bible passage in which Jesus walks on the water of the Sea of Galilee. The purpose of this background chapter is to acquaint us with the events immediately preceding the water-walking episode. Understanding the event's context in this way will help us understand the disciples' responses to their own successes and failures, and it will help us comprehend some of the baggage—emotional, mental, and physical—that they brought with them to the event; it also will help us discover how God works with those who really know Him.

The issues raised in this section will not exhibit a strictly chronological relationship any more than several months in our own lives can be understood strictly chronologically. The issues that arise, the thoughts, feelings and temptations that accompany them, and the decisions that are finally made about them have a relationship, but not through a simple sequential connection. Ultimately, the framework through which we see all of the issues of life, along with the thoughts, feelings and impressions that accompany the issues, is the determining factor. What is the framework, or grid, that will deliver us in a time of trial? We will begin laying the foundation for that grid in this section. Right thinking is the first step toward healthy emotions and spiritual victory.

Early in His ministry, Jesus selected twelve men from the multitudes that were following Him to participate in a closer, more intimate walk with Him. These twelve men are later called apostles, or "sent ones," because they would be sent out to minister on their own by the authority that Jesus would delegate to them. These apostles portray for us what a "disciple" is, namely, a follower of Jesus committed to being His servant in every aspect of life. That means that we are His Ambassadors, sent on a divine mission every single day of our lives! And all that He requires of us is faithfulness.[14] If we are faithful, we will be adequate;[15] if we are adequate, we will be successful in the mission that He has assigned to us.[16]

Jesus proposes a hard-earned rest

The passage that we are going to consider in our study finds the apostles just returning from an extended, three-month ministry of preaching and performing miracles. They had healed the sick, raised the dead and cleansed lepers.[17] Not a bad experience for a bunch of fishermen! Upon their return, they were as tired as they were excited about what God had done through them. As they reported to Jesus all that they had done, He recognized their weary state and invited them to get away with Him for a little leisure time. Jesus intended this rest time to renew them physically as well as spiritually. These first disciples learned early that **there is nothing like being in the presence of Jesus to bring life into focus, to renew one's strength, and to confirm one's purpose.**

This should catch the attention of those who are seeking God's help in their own trials. When you feel confused, vulnerable because of your weary condition, or aimless, having no real goal for your life, it may be that you are in desperate need of an extended time in the presence of Jesus. Jesus was the one who recommended this time together and initiated the retreat to a deserted place. Jesus' presence is never an idle presence: He cannot be present and not be involved in supplying

---

[14] 2 Timothy 2:2b.
[15] 2 Timothy 2:2c; cf. also 2 Corinthians 3:5-6.
[16] 2 Corinthians 12:9-10; 2 Corinthians 4:7-11.
[17] Matthew 10:1-4, 8-9.

our needs out of His infinite goodness. Hence, to learn to be with Him is to learn how to trust Him to act on our behalf according to His precious and magnificent promises.

Unfortunately for the disciples, this leisure time was interrupted by a vast multitude of people seeking instruction and healing from Jesus. Most of us can understand what the disciples were experiencing. Do you remember the last time you were interrupted at dinnertime by the phone call of a solicitor? When you answered the call, you found it difficult to end the conversation, which only the solicitor was interested in sustaining. You were ready for a wonderful dinner with your family, but now this caller had stolen your time and changed a relaxing evening into one filled with tension and resentment. You do not even know the person calling, but you now dislike him anyway, right? The disciples' dilemma was similar. Their leisure time with Jesus was interrupted, and their response to this invasion of their privacy was anything but spiritual. Resentment arose; bitterness took root.

This was only the beginning of their disappointment, however. Their situation deteriorated quickly. After they had listened to Jesus teach the multitude all day long, they were called upon to feed this huge crowd. Not only had their quiet time, their personal time with Jesus, been interrupted, they were now being asked to serve the very ones who had stolen from them their opportunity to be alone with Him. We can deduce that the disciples resented this intrusion into their private time with Jesus from the fact that their hearts became spiritually hardened.[18] What is plain is that at whatever time they first chose to respond selfishly, for some time afterward darkness covered their souls like a cloudy night covers the earth. As a result, they were not able to gain any insight into the nature of

[18] Mark 6:52.

life, into their Lord, or into their own hearts. *Their spiritual state directly affected their receptivity and their understanding.*

We must not picture the disciples as mean, angry, harsh or troublesome people, however. Hardness of heart refers to the spiritual sensitivity of a person toward God and may be entirely hidden from the naked eye. As cancer makes the body unsound, even though there may be no perceptible outward signs until the very end of physical life, hardness of heart makes the spiritual life unsound, even though there may not be any outward signs of that unsoundness. God's common grace can keep a person moral, disciplined in the things of God, and involved in personal ministry without generating a spiritual life within. **We must never assume that our conformation to Christianity is the same thing as our transformation to Christ.** A Christian is not someone who does Christian activities. A Christian is a person who has trusted Jesus for the forgiveness of sins and the gift of eternal life. Having trusted Jesus for these things, that person now has a relationship with the resurrected Christ, and, through that relationship, the capacity to live on a different spiritual plane altogether.

Only when a Christian walks in the light of God's Word can he have fellowship with God and with His only Son, Jesus Christ.[19] Our ability to learn about God and life is vastly increased as we consistently walk with God.[20] He never intended to keep knowledge away from us, contrary to Satan's suggestion to Eve in the Garden of Eden.[21] Rather, He always has wanted us to obtain it as we maintain a right relationship with Him.[22]

---

[19] 1 John 1:7.
[20] Cf. Colossians 1:9-12.
[21] Genesis 3:5-6.
[22] Cf. Genesis 3:1-22; Proverbs 1:7 and John 17:3, 17.

The consequences of a hardened heart

The striking fact is that **the disciples' hardness of heart must have created an impenetrable barrier around their souls**, even during the distribution of the food and the gathering of the twelve baskets filled with leftovers. This hardness blocked their receptivity and voided all spiritual sensitivity. They were walking as though they had no spiritual life in them at all. They were responding in exactly the way that an unbeliever would have responded.[23]

Assuming that each disciple could carry enough food to feed ten people at a time, each disciple would have had to go back and forth from Jesus to the crowd over forty times to feed the five thousand men before them! We should not forget that they started with five loaves (or biscuits) and two fish, only enough food for a young boy to eat by himself. How could the disciples not be impressed with the magnitude of this miracle? And to end with more food than they had when they began! How deplorable the state of their hearts must have been! But such a deplorable state can be the experience of any believer. When we refuse to respond properly to the trials that God brings into our lives, we demonstrate to everyone that we have cut ourselves off from the sovereign God who brought the trial in the first place and who intended to wonderfully sustain us throughout the difficulty that He Himself brought.

Consider carefully what we know of the disciples' circumstances. They could not have been closer to Jesus, physically speaking; they could not have been any more involved in ministry; they could not have been following Jesus' instructions in the distribution of the food to the crowd any more meticulously. Nevertheless, their hearts were not in it.

[23] Ephesians 4:17-19; cf. 1 Corinthians 3:1-3.

They were receiving no spiritual benefit in spite of all the privileges that they were experiencing first hand. They were in a spiritual state that prohibited their spiritual receptivity and growth.

Their experience shows us two things: that "Christian ministries" can be carried out with hardened hearts, and that any ministry undertaken without a spiritually submissive heart is incapable of producing spiritual benefits in its participants. Preachers, teachers, Sunday school superintendents, Sunday school teachers and helpers, child care volunteers, evangelists, elders and deacons can be involved in Christian ministry for years without the slightest bit of spiritual growth. Sacrifices for the sake of Christian ministry can spring from a fleshly, self-centered heart, making "fruit-checking" by those observing their lives a blindly presumptuous exercise.

During the past thirty years of ministry, I have found that there are a great many Christians who "serve" Jesus just as the disciples were doing. They desire to be close to Jesus; they desire to be involved in ministry for Him; they desire to be obedient to His Word as found in the Bible, but in the end they feel empty, distant, and even isolated from THE PERSON of the Savior. There is a cloud upon their souls. Instead of experiencing the joy of the Lord as their motivating impulse, they are urged onward by guilt. They know what they should do and that conviction alone presses them forward.

We must remember that our relationship with Him not only secures our eternal destiny, but it is also capable of abundantly sustaining us until we reach that destiny. The first it does automatically; the second it does conditionally. Being in Christ secures our destiny unconditionally;[24] Christ living in us, a

---

[24] John 5:24; 10:27-29.

condition that is realized only when we walk by faith,[25] provides the spiritual victory that we long to experience while we journey toward eternity.[26]

The disciples had hardened hearts. Is it possible that you do too? Their hardness took away their sense of God's presence, their awe of His power and the privilege of their service to Him. The presence of the multitude (their immediate trial) led them to take their eyes off Jesus, the divine solution, and place them on the problem (the multitude). As long as anyone focuses solely upon his problem, he will have distress. As long as the disciples focused on their problem, they lost all sense and all wonder of Jesus' power to minister to them in their circumstance. And as long as they focused on the multitude as an unwanted problem, they could not imagine that God might have intended this crowd as an opportunity for their (the disciples) service to Him. A hardened heart creates a needy soul.

Disappointments reveal our self-centeredness

Why were the disciples responding so carnally? They were experiencing what I call "broken expectations." They had hoped to spend some quality time with Jesus. It would not be surprising if the disciples even thought that they deserved this special time with Jesus in light of the sacrificial service they had just rendered. When the multitudes showed up, the disciples reacted. Most likely, they kept their true feelings inside; nevertheless, they were miserable throughout this whole day of ministry.

---

[25] Ephesians 3:16-17.
[26] 2 Corinthians 4:16-18.

They probably found this time boring and spiritually ineffective because **they could not see beyond the disappointment that they were experiencing**. They knew that they were not being ministered to in the way they had hoped during this time, and perhaps they supposed that no one else was being ministered to, either. They were so disappointed that when it came time to eat, they suggested that Jesus send the multitude away. We can imagine that they were hoping to end the evening with some private time with Jesus around dinner. But the interruption of their plans was not over yet. They were not going to be able to manipulate the situation to provide for themselves what they really wanted.

Have you ever noticed that, when trials come upon us, we expend an enormous amount of mental, emotional, and physical energy trying to manipulate our situation just to gain the smallest bit of personal satisfaction? That we become more frustrated and increasingly irritable when we find we are not able to change our circumstances in the slightest? That the only reason we continue to endure the trial before us is that there is some promise of relief or blessing on the other side of our trial? So we begrudgingly tolerate the trial because there is nothing else we can do. Life is full of trials, and it will never be a consistently pleasant, fulfilling experience for the selfish: God has rigged life so that fulfillment is found only in self-abandonment to the will and ways of God. The selfish will find that lasting peace, fulfillment and contentment are always elusive.

How many times can you recall that life has not gone the way that you wished it would go? Although you were an all-American athlete, you developed knee problems your senior year and your dreams of playing professional football slipped away. Your parents got a divorce and your life became as severed as the relationship between your parents. Your spouse was caught cheating on you, and now you feel that your trust in him or her has been irretrievably lost. Maybe one of your parents died prematurely and you felt abandoned and lost. Or maybe your parents did not give you the love that you so desperately wanted, leaving you feeling insecure and on your own. Maybe it was the loss of a job or of a loved one that has brought devastating consequences into your life. Or maybe there were sicknesses or violence or a host of catastrophes that have changed the course of your life permanently. How are these things to be handled? What response is to be given to such disruptions and heartaches? What can we do when our dreams and desires, our very lives, are shattered?

We can learn the answer to these questions by looking at the passages before us. How did the disciples respond when life did not go their way? They had a choice to make. They could respond in dependence upon the infinitely wise providence of a sovereign and loving God, believing that their physical and spiritual refreshment would be accomplished in God's time and in God's way. Or they could respond like selfish, pouting children who were unhappy because life was not going their way. Living like selfish, demanding children in a grown-up world will never bring happiness. Unfortunately, the disciples chose the latter path, a choice made by multitudes of Christians today.

As you contemplate the disciples' dilemma in Matthew 14:13-21, notice that their hardened response did not help them in the least. It did not somehow transform them into patient, caring, sensitive people ready to serve others. It did not help them deal with their broken expectations. It did not make their day easier to bear. Nor did it provide any insight into life. Their response was a total waste (except for it being used as a bad example for us!). **Bad responses will not deliver in the day of trouble; they will only increase the pain, disappointment and despair that is being experienced.** A bad response is any response that is contrary to the desired will of God.

Two foundational truths help reorient our focus

How do you respond when life does not go your way? You too have a choice. Either you can trust in the goodness of God, like the psalmist,[27] or you can reveal to the world your own self-centeredness by the telltale character traits that nearly everyone recognizes. Most Christians are familiar with, or have memorized, Romans 8:28: "All things work together for good to them that love God, for them that are called according to His purpose." We propagate this truth theologically, but hardly ever practice it in any consistent way from day to day.

When was the last time you noticed someone focusing upon one of his broken expectations and explaining the ways that God used it in his life for good? When was the last time YOU focused upon a serious disillusionment or heartache, one of your own broken dreams, one of your own unfulfilled desires, but instead of dwelling upon what you wished had happened, you praised God for what He did in your life that was good through it all? The truth is, God is working in the trial you are facing to bring about something very, very good in your life. In the midst of loss and heartache, difficulty and disappointment, God is orchestrating your circumstances and supplying you with unbelievable grace to change you at the very core of your being so you can experience more of Him and His blessings. But instead of leading us to trust in God more fully, our trials offer

[27] Psalm 27:13.

our hardened hearts excuses for not trusting in God at all. This is the reason why many Christians know how to quote Romans 8:28, but few experience the sweetness of life that comes from the truths of that verse.

The disciples knew that God was sovereign in His control over all things.[28] They knew that He loved them and had good plans for their lives.[29] But they were not trusting God to fulfill these commitments to them in the midst of their trial, at the time they really needed those blessings most.

In reality, many Christians' lives are childish in the extreme. Children may pout, may get angry, may cry and whine when they do not get their way, but they usually get over it very quickly. Not so with many adult Christians! They live with their hurts, refusing to let them go, refusing to get over them. They refuse to obey the Scriptures that command them to "give thanks in all things for this is the will of God for you in Christ Jesus!" This is the second truth that will reorient our focus in difficult times.

Look up 1 Thessalonians 5:18 in your Bible. The words "in all things" are in the emphatic position in the Greek sentence. *In all things*, not just in those that we readily can see are positive, we have a command from God resting upon us, a divine requirement to give a certain response. "In all things, *give thanks*." Again, let me point out that the response that is enjoined upon us in this passage is not merely a suggestion! It is a command: "Give thanks!" It is disobedience not to do so.[30] But rather than be obedient, many Christians actually nurture their "life wounds" as though they were battle scars symbolizing heroic action on their part. With these scars they have indeed

---

[28] Psalm 103:19; Proverbs 16:1, 4, 9; Isaiah 14:26-27; 43:13; etc.
[29] Lamentations 3:22-23; Jeremiah 29:11.
[30] The disciples knew all this from the Old Testament. Compare Psalms 9, 27 and 73, for example.

Background to Our Passage

become part of a prestigious group of people, namely, the surviving victims of life's everyday trials, mislabeled "tragedies" by many. But by nurturing these wounds they separate themselves from Jesus. **Wounded people are not dead people.**[31] **And until we die, we are not ready to live.**[32]

"To die to self" is to reckon upon the truth that our hearts are so misguided, confused and distorted, being full of sinful self-centeredness, that any claims our hearts make for personal rights or individual needs not grounded in the express declarations of Scripture, are false and must not be given a moment's validity. No one can follow God and listen to his own unaided heart at the same time. Through the entire Bible, the heart of every man, including the heart of the Christian, is, only and always, opposed to God and His will. Every thought, feeling or act coming from within the heart of man is "evil and that continually."[33] So, when our hearts tell us what our rights are, or how we should think, act or feel when we are mistreated, they can only lead us astray.

These two passages, Romans 8:28 and 1 Thessalonians 5:18, were written by the apostle Paul who experienced more suffering than most people ever will have to endure.[34] They must form part of our grid: when trials come or when they linger, we must remember these truths and trust God to sustain us with all of His blessings. Although the disciples were dealing with difficult circumstances, God expected them to relate those situations to the truth that they had been taught in the past and to trust in His faithfulness to "work all things together for good." He expects the same from us as well.

---

[31] Romans 6:11.
[32] Romans 6:12-13.
[33] Cf., Genesis 6:5; Jeremiah 17:9; Isaiah 64:6; Romans 7:14-23; Galatians 5:16-17.
[34] 2 Corinthians 11:23-33.

I have often wondered about something. When I hear a Christian talk about his "wounds" and his "hurts" and his "scars" from events that happened in his life, some times long ago, I wonder, "Who has kept these wounds from healing?" It cannot be Jesus, because He is the Great Physician, who came "to proclaim release to the captives and recovery of sight to the blind, to set free those who are downtrodden."[35] "A battered reed He will not break off, and a smoldering wick He will not put out...."[36] It can not be the universal Body of Christ, the Church, since this is hardly the testimony that the evangelical Church wishes to give to the world, namely, a Savior who can not deliver, a Great Physician who can not heal, an Omnipotent God who is powerless over the crises and difficulties that one has experienced in the past, a Wonderful Counselor who is ineffectual in His counseling. Who needs this kind of "savior?" And as far as the "church" is concerned, when it has become little more than another support group, who needs it when there already are so many support groups to choose from? Redundancy is the need of a confused mind.

Who, then, would want to keep the wounds that Christians have from healing? There are only three: *the world* who knows of no Savior who can deliver; *the Devil* who opposes the Savior who desires to deliver; and *the flesh* which does not want the Savior to deliver for selfish reasons. Where do you fit, Dear Reader? Are you following the advice of a world that has no place for a supernatural Savior who can directly intervene in your life? Are you being directly assaulted by the Evil One who is trying to convince you that Jesus cannot help you? Is it your own self-centered heart that refuses to deny itself and trust Jesus to fulfill His Word to you? Jesus Himself said, "All things are possible to

---

[35] Luke 4:18.
[36] Matthew 12:20.

him who believes."[37] Will you repent of the path you have chosen up to this point in your life and come to Jesus, who alone can heal you?

The disciples' hardness of heart teaches us the futility of Christian service—and even the futility of living life itself—apart from a dependence upon the Lord. Disappointments and pain, devastating losses, all come our way by the hands of an infinitely wise God who brings pressure upon us from all sides in order to mold us into the image of His own Son.[38] He has to give us a distaste for all the things and relationships in the world before we can appreciate His sweetness.[39] We are so stubborn and blind—so hard-hearted—that we will continue to run to every conceivable support but God, until we discover for ourselves that there are no other options that will support us. **Our hurts remain because the cure we expect from the world, only God can give.**

Preparing ourselves to experience God's deliverance

Is it not interesting that the Lord Jesus Christ, who knows the heart of man and is able to rightly critique every motive and intention,[40] does not rebuke the disciples during this whole day of ministry? How could they have denied their hardness of heart if they had heard His gentle, piercing rebuke? Yet, He allowed them to persist in their hardness and miss the lessons they really needed to learn, miss the comfort that He wanted to give, and miss the deliverance that He alone could provide. He knows

---

[37] Mark 9:23.
[38] Jeremiah 18:4; Cf., Romans 8:29 and 2 Corinthians 3:18.
[39] 1 John 2:15-17.
[40] Proverbs 16:2; cf. Hebrews 4:12-13.

where we are as well. We must draw near to God,[41] trusting Him to meet the needs of our souls. We must be willing to have Him completely remove our hardness of heart and grant us His resources to respond in a way in which we are not capable of responding ourselves. He is asking for a response from us that will bring Him glory and praise.

Hardness of heart is a culpable state. The disciples teach us that a hardened heart can be possessed by someone involved in ministry; it can be true of someone who is serving others; it can be descriptive of someone who is at a place of service where Jesus is being glorified. But because of the hardness of heart, the voice of God is being stifled. The lessons that God has for the hard-hearted are being missed. Experience is God's way of reinforcing the truths that He has revealed in the Bible. The person who knows the principles of Scripture sees these principles tattooed on the events of life. He finds himself thinking, as he observes life around him, "Of course! God said that this consequence would follow that choice." Yet, on the other hand, a hardened heart dulls our understanding and even makes us forgetful of God's truths, because the ministry of the Holy Spirit within our hearts is being quenched by unbelief.[42]

It does not matter in the least what the circumstances were that occasioned a person's hardness of heart. If we were together, I would have you, the reader, repeat that last sentence until it is firmly ingrained in your memory! Once we pull the shades down on our souls, for whatever reasons, we will not be able to see out. And as long as we are closed off from God's divine light, we will grope in the darkness, falling again and again over the very provisions and blessings that God wanted to use to draw us closer to Himself.

---

[41] James 4:8-10.
[42] Cf., Matthew 13:19; Hebrews 5:12; 1Thess. 5:19-22.

Background to Our Passage

Just as the disciples had to struggle against being hard hearted, we have to struggle against the same temptation. We all have the same battle going on inside of us. **One deception of a hardened heart is that it is often quite tender toward others while it is very much estranged from God and His love.** So, the real issue is, "How close am I to God? Is He the support of my life?"

There may be issues that you need to address before you continue this study. Will you humble yourself before the Lord and ask Him to search your heart to see if there is any lack of conformity to His revealed will there?[43] Sooner or later, we must confess and repent of all of the sins that we have chosen to harbor, so that God can bury them in the deepest part of the sea.[44] Sometimes in life, our gracious Lord will allow us to proceed with our lives without addressing some sin that resides within. This is what Jesus allowed the disciples to do as they proceeded from the feeding of the 5,000 to the miraculous event of Jesus walking on the water. At other times, however, Jesus rebuked the disciples' sin and expected them to confess it and deal with it immediately and appropriately. This is how Jesus deals with Peter after he refuses to accept His prediction of His coming suffering, death and resurrection.[45] If you will be willing to make a 180 degree turn, God will make known to you what His will is, and He will give you the ability to carry it out for His glory.[46] Then you will have success;[47] then you will find the happiness, fulfillment and purpose that you seek.[48]

---

[43] Psalm 139:23-24.
[44] 1 John 1:9; Luke 24:47; Psalm 103:10-12
[45] Matthew 16:21-27.
[46] John 7:17.
[47] Joshua 1:8.
[48] Jeremiah 29:11.

So take a moment and be circumspect. Let your life and all your relationships and activities pass before your mind's eye. Ask God to point out any sin or habit or selfish disposition that you might be harboring within. Do not try to excuse yourself or rationalize away what God's Spirit shows you. If there is anything exposed which is contrary to God's Word, it needs to be confessed;[49] if restitution is required, it needs to be given;[50] in all humility, forgiveness needs to be sought from any offended party.[51] In all of this, trust God for His strength to accomplish His will in your own heart and, through your actions, towards others in your life. If the disciples had done this, they would have been well prepared to handle the crisis that God was about to bring into their lives.

Now we are ready to begin our study of the text of Matthew 14:22-33, and learn how "to live"—really live, and not just exist—through the crises that come into our lives.

---

[49] 1 John 1:9.
[50] Matthew 5:23-24.
[51] Luke 17:3-4; Galatians 6:1ff.

~Living~ Through Crises

PRINCIPLE ONE: *Our most pressing need is not more time to work through our trials; our most pressing need is a new life to handle our trials!*

The disciples already knew enough to respond properly in the trials that were coming upon them. But Jesus had so much more to teach them. Their experiences, as ours are, were fashioned to teach them profound truths about God's care and His all-sufficient provisions. So as we look back upon their trials, we can glean from them truths that will encourage us today as they should have encouraged the disciples nearly two thousand years ago.

Maybe the most important truth that you will learn in this book is this: **the trial that has come upon you is NOT the problem. The real problem is the condition of your heart!** This will always be the fundamental truth, and we must face it honestly. Again and again we will come back to it in our study. Our objective in a trial must not be to change our circumstances or to use all of our energy to remove ourselves from them; our objective is to trust God to change us: to renew our minds by implanting in us His perspective about our trial; to give us godly emotions so that we may experience His love and joy throughout the duration of our trials; and to enable our wills to respond consistently according to our new perspective and emotions. In short, we need a new life (a whole new capacity) to give glory to God by responding as we should. This new life comes from Jesus who lives within us through the inner ministry of the Holy Spirit. The One who has peace in the midst of turmoil, joy in the midst of sorrow, patience in the midst of obstacles and suffering, love in the midst of hatred, strength at the time of greatest weakness, and hope in the darkest hour is the Person who wants to pass on His life to us. This transference (experience) of life, this appropriation of Jesus' supernatural resources from the Holy Spirit, must be our goal at all times. Everything else is secondary at best. Your trial is God's providentially sent opportunity for you to learn to trust Him, regardless of what happens to your world.

The disciples' terrifying experience in a storm immediately followed a trial that they had failed miserably. (We discussed this trial in the Background chapter above.) The words that Matthew chooses to introduce the disciples' new experience should arrest our attention: Matthew 14:22 begins, "And immediately." The disciples had little time to dwell upon the miracle of the feeding of the five thousand or upon their inadequate response to that trial. No time was given to "work through" their disappointment; no time was granted to "deal with" their resentment; no time was given to "talk through" their "hurt."

Jesus knew all about their hardness of heart.[52] Given this understanding of their spiritual state, He also knew the sense of terror, helplessness and devastation that they could experience at their next trial. So, if the correction of their past failure was the critical issue that needed to be addressed, surely Jesus would have done that immediately and not allowed the opportunity to pass. Because He did not do this, He would have us understand that their new trial was not caused by their failure to properly respond to His all-day ministry to the multitude and the feeding of the 5,000. Nor was the first matter of importance dealing with the disciples' failure to trust Him. Their new trial was a new opportunity to respond to a new dilemma; it was not a veiled warning to correct their failure in the past before they could be

---

[52] This is proven by Mark 6:52.

delivered from their present danger. Neither was their new trial a divine threat that the disciples were supposed to recognize.

There was no time given to the disciples to linger at the site of the miracle because hardness of heart and the spiritual blindness that accompanies it, even in the believer, are not self-curable. **Our receptivity is determined by the state of our heart, not by the length of time truth confronts it.** Consequently, change can come immediately if we "humble [ourselves] under the mighty hand of God, [by] casting all [our] cares upon Him for He cares for [us]."[53] Although meditation on additional Biblical truth—God's will for our lives—does facilitate proper responses, it is not a requirement. Faith is what pleases God; He delights in rewarding it whenever it is expressed. So if we know what God wants from us, that truth is enough to act upon, and we can trust God to provide the resources we need to act. We will seldom have all the answers we would like to have before making a decision. If we trust God for what we know at a given moment, He will continue leading us by revealing more and more of His will to us.

If we really needed time to "work through" the trial we are facing (or some past failure that we have experienced) in order to give a proper response to God, then God surely must be held accountable for bringing one trial after the next upon us. The fact of the matter is just the opposite. We do not need more time to respond to God properly; we need a "new life" to respond properly, one that has already been implanted within us and ready to be accessed by simple faith. **If we refuse to live by this new life within us, we will never conclude that we have had enough time to respond appropriately to God.** To understand that this is true, ask yourself this question, "How long have I been held in bondage to some devastating emotion because I

---

[53] 1 Peter 5:6-7.

have been convinced that 'I have not had enough time' to work through my problem yet?" As long as we put off responding as God requires us to respond, our turmoil remains.

Our actual "readiness" to handle a trial does not determine what God sends into our life or when He will send the next trial to us. We have the potential to be "ready in season and out of season."[54] So, if our hearts become hardened and we wander from God, the trials He has planned for us are more crushing, because the carnal state of our hearts simply cannot bear the weight. If our hearts were right, the trial would have proven to be, seemingly, light[55] because, when the Lord is our Shepherd, we have no want.[56] That is the goal of our study together: to experience His tender care "even though [we must] walk through the Valley of the Shadow of Death" … " in the presence of [our] enemies."[57]

Another reason we do not need more time to respond, as we tend to suppose, is that the crisis that we are experiencing is not unique to us. God assures us that there are Christians all over the world who are enduring the very same trials that we are,[58] and some are enduring joyfully much worse.[59] Our trial, then, is not a special case; more time is not needed; others can easily understand our dilemma because they have or are experiencing exactly the same kind of difficulty that we are experiencing.

A person may feel that he needs more time to respond properly because the trial is especially severe, but God will not lower His standards for that person while He requires the rest of

---

[54] 2 Timothy 4:2.
[55] Matthew 11:28-30.
[56] Psalm 23:1.
[57] Psalm 23:4, 5.
[58] 1 Peter 1:13-21; 2:18-23; 4:12-19; 5:6-11. See also the first two chapters of the book of Job.
[59] Every reader ought to obtain a magazine that chronicles the suffering of Christians around the world, and then compare what they have been asked to endure by God to what others are enduring. The *Voice of the Martyrs* is an excellent resource.

the world to respond immediately in living righteous and holy lives. The standard is the same for all:

> "Therefore, gird your minds for action, keep sober in spirit, fix your hope completely on the grace to be brought to you at the revelation of Jesus Christ. As obedient children, do not be conformed to the former lusts which were yours in your ignorance, but like the Holy One who called you, be holy yourselves also in all your behavior; because it is written, 'You shall be holy, for I am holy.' And if you address as Father the One who impartially judges according to each man's work, conduct yourselves in fear during the time of your stay upon earth."[60]

But, "I do not feel capable of responding yet"

God can make our trial profitable to us[61] as He protects[62] and sustains[63] us. But make no mistake about it, just as God did not give the disciples time to work through their failure and disappointment, He does not give us time to work through ours either. The reason is simple: the issue is not that we need more time to overcome our trial. The issue is that **we do not have the innate ability to overcome the trial at all!** Getting all the time in the world will not help the *incapable*! Getting the best advice in the world will not produce success in those *incapable* of carrying out the advice! Getting the best encouragement in the world will not change the life of the person who is *incapable* of maintaining

---

[60] 1 Peter 1:13-17.
[61] James 1:2-4.
[62] Philippians 4:6-7.
[63] Philippians 4:10-13.

personal hope. If we persist in our attempt to conquer our trials with the wisdom and resources of man, then Jesus died needlessly, since He did not come to give a turbo boost to our fleshly engines. He came to provide a whole other engine to empower our lives. The proper response that God is looking for is one that trusts Him to intervene in our lives according to His own promises in order to provide all that we need to overcome our trials. Do you understand your own incapacity?

Nothing short of the experience of a new life will prove effective in handling the trials before us. Even the experience of miracles will not prove sufficient to deliver our hearts from the turmoil occasioned by the trial before us. Jesus had just fed over 5,000 people with a sack lunch. There were twelve baskets full of food left over. The disciples saw this miracle first hand, and yet were untouched by it. It is apparent, then, that **a miracle has no special efficacy upon the human heart just because it is an extraordinary event.** If it did, the disciples would have been compelled to respond to Jesus, the Lord of all sufficiency. If it did, Jesus' miracles would have produced many, many more believers, because His ministry was full of miracles.[64]

If miracles are not efficacious even though they are extraordinary events, is it logical to expect any other religious experience *per se* to soften and energize the heart toward God? **Experience may give a great assortment of temporary aids to the believer:** encouragement, motivation, challenge and hope. **But only God Himself changes and empowers the heart to respond triumphantly in our great trials.**[65] All we can do is yield ourselves[66] into the hands of the divine Potter,[67] trusting

---

[64] John 2:23-25; 20:30-31.
[65] 2 Corinthians 3:18.
[66] Romans 6:13.
[67] Jeremiah 18:1-4; Romans 9:20.

Him to produce all the transformation (change!)[68] that He desires to see in us. We must not look to seminars, retreats or other blessings to change us; we must yield ourselves into the hands of God. Then as He provides to us by faith what He promises, we then step out again in faith to address the world with the resources He has supplied to us.

Although God does not wait on us to respond as we should, He does offer all we need to endure successfully the trial before us. This point will be demonstrated later in our study. It is obvious that it is easier to handle a devastating trial when we are emotionally at peace and have strong confidence in God than it is when we are stubbornly independent of God and emotionally in turmoil.[69] We must remember that God never intended us to bear the weight of our trials. Jesus is meant to bear all the weight for us. So, if we enter a trial and become overwhelmed by it, there can be only one reason for our failure: we are not allowing Jesus to carry on His own shoulders our burdens. If, when He returns to earth, the government of the whole world will be on His shoulders,[70] can we not trust Him to bear our little burden now? **He died in order to bear the burden of our every sin;[71] He now lives within our hearts by the power of God's Spirit to bear the burden of our every struggle.**[72]

As I have pointed out earlier, there is no indication that the trial that the disciples were about to face had anything to do with the sin that they had just committed. It would be wrong to think that trials only come upon us because of our sin. Some do, of course. But trials are not used for divine discipline alone. If

---

[68] Romans 12:2. Notice that the verb is passive. God transforms us; we don't change ourselves!
[69] Principle #5 will be devoted to this premise.
[70] Isaiah 9:6.
[71] 1 Peter 2:24a.
[72] 1 Peter 2:24b-25.

they were, Jesus should never have had any trials. The disciples' past was past. It in no way predetermined how they would respond in their new trial. Peter proves this irrefutably. Their past did not limit what they could experience if they chose to respond in faith. Jesus was now asking them to look to Him and be delivered from their present trial. He was asking them to trust Him so that He could show them, by His own hand, great and mighty things that they were incapable of doing by themselves. God is asking the same from you and me. He is inviting us to break the bonds of our past by exercising faith in Him. If we do, He will be faithful to fulfill all of His promises to us.

The trials we face are part of God's divine plan to bring us to the place of self-abandonment and divine trust. The answer to life is not provided by anything found in ordinary life.[73] The answer to life is in God alone. **The trials that we are currently facing are indirect divine prescriptions for our spiritual healing and maturity.** God is working through each one of our trials to bring us into a full experience of His own love for us and of His wonderful provisions for our lives.

Trials, then, are not a sign of divine displeasure as much as a sign of continuing divine love, one that seeks to draw us to the remedy for our present miseries. In this way only, the hopeless will have hope; the weak will find strength; the empty will be filled; the overwhelmed will conquer; the inadequate will be sufficient. Our lack will be abundantly supplied by the infinite resources of the God who loves us.[74] What Jesus told Paul is true for us as well: "My grace is sufficient for you, for power is perfected in weakness."[75] And, likewise, Paul's response to Jesus' revelation ought to be our response too: "Most

---

[73] See the Book of Ecclesiastes.
[74] 2 Corinthians 12:7-9.
[75] 2 Corinthians 12:9a.

gladly, therefore, I will rather boast about my weaknesses, that the power of Christ may dwell in me."[76] Our need is not more time to work through our trial; our need is to experience the life that can give us immediate spiritual victory. Why should we wait any longer?

[76] 2 Corinthians 12:9b.

II

PRINCIPLE TWO: *God will lead us into trials, situations that we do not want to experience, in order to sensitize us to our continuing, natural resistance to His will and to uncover our false pride.*

The crisis before you is not about what you may lose (or have lost). If God deems it best, He can easily prevent the loss. If He deems a temporary loss best, He can later restore it to you two-fold[77] or a hundred-fold.[78] **The crisis before you is about YOU!** God wants to reveal to you some powerful truths about your own heart, His continuing love for you, and His sufficiency to supply your deepest needs.

We often receive this revelation about ourselves at times and in circumstances that we never want to experience. And our first response is usually something like this: "Well, I responded poorly only because I was under such stress. I am not really like that." But that is exactly God's point. The stress of our trial has only revealed what is really true of us. The trial that came our way did not force us to respond poorly; the trial only revealed the nature of our hearts and what we are really like in ourselves.

Notice in Matthew 14:22 that Jesus "necessitated" (made) the disciples to embark into the boat. The force of the term implies that the disciples did not want to go. Jesus had to coerce them; He had to compel them; He had to make them get into the boat and proceed on ahead of Him. Jesus set a path before them that they did not want to travel. This path He laid for their training, for their development, and for their maturity. This is the reason

---

[77] Job 42:10-17.
[78] Mark 10:30.

for your trial as well. To try to avoid the path or to respond inappropriately in the path is to miss God's process of bringing us closer to Himself by making our own inadequacies evident to us.

The disciples' hesitation to obey

Now we are not told why the disciples did not want to get into the boat and leave. Maybe they did not want to go because they simply did not want to leave Jesus' presence. **Even when our hearts are in their coldest state, we are still warmed by and drawn to God's presence and unchanging love.** Although the disciples were not responding spiritually, they still knew who Jesus was, and that He had always been the answer to every problem they had faced. All they needed to do was return to Him. But would they?

Many Christians are caught in this same trap: they cannot deny who Jesus is, but they follow Him only with great reservation. The sense that an observer gets as he watches the interaction between some Christians and Jesus is that He is someone with whom one can negotiate. His will is not better than anyone else's, so each person should seek his own compromise with Him.

The reasons Christians do not want to follow Him may differ from person to person. Maybe this is part of the reason Jesus said that the first step in being His disciple is to deny oneself.[79] **Self-denial always precedes divine usefulness,[80] and divine usefulness is always an integral part of the transformation process.** Self-denial is the forfeiture to Jesus of

[79] Luke 9:23.
[80] The reference is to Christians being used in the desired will of God.

all rights in order to carry out the Ambassadorship that He has entrusted to us.[81] Jesus commands self-denial from every would-be disciple because residing in the heart of each of us is a continuing disinclination to follow Jesus.[82] This disinclination is always fighting to manifest itself, and it often succeeds in times of trials.[83] When our responses in times of trials surprise us (or others), we are faced with the fact that we really are not the mature people we think we are. Trials peel off the façade that our flesh has worked very hard to create. Without these times of transparency, we would be blinded by the delusion of believing in our own adequacy.

Maybe the disciples were just being practical, and this was their reason for not wanting to leave Jesus and precede Him to the other side of the lake. They may have been concerned about how Jesus would get to the other side without them. One has to wonder in what way Jesus explained how He would follow them later. Indeed, how would He come by Himself alone? Whether they were offering themselves as humble servants or whether they had a too elevated view of their own importance (e.g., Jesus surely could not get across without us!), there is no way of telling. But we must remember that their spiritual state at this moment was anything but humble. It would not be surprising if the disciples were thinking too highly of themselves, especially after their successful ministry of healing and preaching. This pride was certainly true of them later in their ministry.[84]

Maybe the disciples did not want to leave because they were concerned about the uncertain, threatening weather conditions. Maybe the wind had just begun to pick up as it was getting dark.

---

[81] 2 Corinthians 5:20.
[82] Galatians 5:16-17.
[83] Malachi 3:13-15.
[84] Cf. Matthew 18:1. Note especially the context of the parallel passage in Luke 22:24!

Surely Jesus did not want them to attempt to cross the lake in stormy conditions! Surely this would be contrary to common sense, and much more so to divine wisdom! Is it not true that we often think we know more than God? Every reticence to obey God's Word and follow Jesus that wells up within us comes from pride, the terrible sin that seeks to dethrone God at every turn.

We also should add to this picture the possibility that their agitation might have sprung from their understanding that their hearts had not been right during the feeding of the 5,000. And now Jesus was sending them away. Guilt is an awful thing to bear, and it is compounded when the guilty party intentionally turns away from the path of forgiveness because of his own pride.

Their emotional state worsens

Whatever reason they had entertained for wanting to stay with Jesus, it did not prove convincing to Jesus. He compelled them to follow a plan (His plan) contrary to their own desires. The disciples were experiencing a very uneasy feeling, a churning within, a nauseous feeling that all was not right. They must have thought, "Surely this feeling of uneasiness cannot be a sign that we are in the will of God. We have always thought the will of God came with divine peace. Where is this incomprehensible calm if this is the will of God? How could a decision that creates such an unsettling of our souls be of God?" They probably never considered the possibility that their lack of peace may have been the result of their own rebellion toward God, not a result of what He was asking them to do!

If their hardness of heart had earlier made them apathetic and indifferent, as we might expect it to have done, that state of affairs had come to an end. Their emotions were now highly agitated, and they were experiencing considerable frustration because they were not getting their way. **Their troubled emotions were caused by their refusal to fully resign themselves to the truth that Jesus' will is always best.** This natural disinclination resides within us all. Like we do so often, the disciples were fighting to have their own way in this matter. Thinking their way was surely best, they became very troubled when they could not have it. Could there be any clearer manifestation of sinful pride?

The trial that you are facing may have been forced upon you, as it was the disciples. Or your trial may be the result of some inappropriate decision that you made. Regardless of the cause of your trial, it is an experience that you would not have chosen for yourself. You wish it had never happened. But God has brought it upon you to reveal your natural resistance to His will and to uncover your false pride.

Your trial is part of God's will for your life.[85] God wants you to face your trial from His perspective and with the resources that He had planned to supply to you. Be committed to the fact that He knows best and, if viewed from an eternal perspective,[86] has only good plans for your life. These good plans will be realized in your life by the divine use of the very trials that have come upon you. This is why we can "consider it all joy when various trials come upon us."[87] Our trials are the means God has ordained to bring about our spiritual maturity. To despair in our trials is to derail God's maturing process,

---

[85] 1 Peter 4:19.
[86] 2 Corinthians 4:16-18.
[87] James 1:2.

forcing us to continue to run a long race without ever getting stronger or wiser in it.[88]

It really is quite simple to uncover what God is trying to do in our lives in times of trials (or at any other time as well). Any trial that we might encounter was fashioned by God either to expose our sin or to demonstrate His power over our sin. If our response to our trial falls short of what God has revealed to us as His will, then the trial is exposing our sin. We must admit that our response was wrong and that we need to trust God to supply to us a response that pleases Him. If we respond properly, God is again encouraging us that He is at work in our lives demonstrating His own power and its sufficiency over every trial. What is God revealing in your life by the trials facing you? Are you responding in a way that falls short of His desired will? Or are you responding in a way that gives evidence of His grace?

---

[88] James 1:3-4.

III. PRINCIPLE THREE: *God may send us into situations in which we feel estranged from Him, when in fact, He is ever watching over us.*

After compelling the disciples to get into the boat and go before Him, Jesus went up on the mountain to pray, having dismissed the crowds that had gathered to hear Him speak. **Just as Jesus did to the disciples, God may send us into situations in which we feel estranged from Him.** God seems to go one way while He sends us in the other. In those situations we may have no sense of His purpose for our lives and no experience of His power. The disciples *went down* into the boat *to paddle* while Jesus *went up* into the mountain *to pray*, the former straining at the oars, the latter sitting at the footstool of the throne of God.

Feeling estranged from Jesus, desperate, and with a growing sense of hopelessness, the disciples were at the point of being overwhelmed. Our feelings about our situation and the reality of our situation may be entirely contradictory. The disciples' plight would have been more endurable if they had known and had held steadfastly to two truths: that Jesus was praying for each disciple and that He was completely in control of their trial in all of its aspects. These two truths are true for us as well today; they will change our feelings of estrangement and desperation into a sense of being loved by God and being confident in His control.

Jesus' prayer of thanksgiving

Jesus went up into the mountain to pray. It goes without saying that if Jesus prayed, so should we. If He saw the need, we should see the need. We do not need to think very long to know what must have been the content of His prayers on this occasion. Surely, thanksgiving constituted part of His prayer. He had just fed over five thousand people with a few loaves and fishes. What a lesson to us this is! **After our greatest spiritual victories or divine blessings, prayer helps keep God in His place and us in ours.** By humbly thanking God in prayer for what He has just done for us, we give no place for pride to manifest itself. God remains the Ruler of the universe, and we remain His unworthy servants,[89] even though He has delighted to work in and through us for His own glory.

We can note the contrast between Jesus' commitment to us in prayer and our fickle commitment to Him. The apostle Paul warns us about allowing ourselves to be "tossed here and there by waves and carried about by every wind of doctrine" so that we do not know which way to face.[90] James, the brother of Jesus, in like fashion, warns us about the instability of a faithless life. If we doubt what God says to us, we are like "the waves of the sea, driven and tossed by the wind."[91] It might have been very discouraging to the disciples that Jesus was not in the boat with them. Yet when they were with Him on shore and He was performing a marvelous miracle before them, they did not value their time with Him very highly! Apparently, the disciples, like we today, wanted to be in God's presence for selfish reasons only. Is it not true that sometimes we do not want to be with

---

[89] Luke 17:7-10.
[90] Ephesians 4:14.
[91] James 1:6.

Jesus to love and enjoy Him? Rather, we want to be with Him to obtain some other blessing that we feel we need. We try to use our relationship with Jesus for selfish reasons. The disciples, after their long arduous ministry, thought they deserved rest, comfort, encouragement, and maybe even praise. What they really needed was to come, once again, face to face with the truth that it is only THE PERSON of Jesus and not His blessings or even His deliverances that will satisfy the human heart!

After the miraculous feeding of the five thousand, Jesus went up the mountain to pray. What is the first thing that we do after we experience a blessing of God? Do we pray? **Does the experience of God's blessings cause us to see ourselves truly?** Or do God's blessings tend to provide us a reason to develop an air about ourselves? **How we respond in our trials reveals how we have been responding to God's blessings in quieter times.**[92] If God's blessings cannot humble us, we can be sure God will use other means, even trials, to bring about this much desired virtue in our lives.

The humility of Jesus is seen in His praying. He prostrated Himself before the Father. If any heart had the right to be raised up, surely it was Jesus'. Peter, too, is a good example of a man who had rightly responded to God's blessings in the past by recognizing that he was completely unworthy of them.[93] **Just as no one is worthy to receive God's blessings, so also no one is worthy to be exempted from His trials.** When you pray, do you mainly focus upon the removal of your trial or of the healing of your "wound?" Or do you pray that God would NOT remove your trial until it has brought you closer to Him? Can you recall

---

[92] Matthew 7:24-27.
[93] Luke 5:4-9.

the last principle in our study? How we pray in times of trials says a lot about us.[94]

Jesus' intercessory prayer

That Jesus' prayer went beyond thanksgiving we can have no doubt. The parallel passage in Mark 6:45-52 reveals more of the content of Jesus' prayer. Verse 48 begins, "And seeing them [the disciples] straining at the oars..." While Jesus was praying, He looked out over the water and saw the disciples in the middle of the lake, straining at the oars. What an awesome picture: **Jesus was praying as He attentively watched over the plight of His disciples!** The Shepherd who felt compassion for shepherdless, lost sheep[95] surely will intercede for His own sheep in their time of trial. What a comfort it is to know that the Shepherd of our souls intercedes for us when we are in the fury of the storms of life! His intercession assures us of God's divine protection and enablement against being overwhelmed in our trials,[96] if we will only learn to trust Him.

He went away alone to pray! Sometimes we have to send even our best friends away so that we can have the intimate discourse with our heavenly Father that we need. Do you get lost in conversation with the heavenly Father when you are alone to pray, or do you just "get lost" when you pray alone? While being alone does allow us to focus, if we do not see God as an intimate, all caring Father, we still may struggle in our prayers as we would when we talk to a stranger. Facility in

---

[94] Acts 4:21-31.
[95] Mark 6:34.
[96] Cf., Luke 22:31-32.

praying grows as our relationship with God develops. And vise versa.

The more intimate the relationship a person has with another, the longer that person desires to sustain it. Jesus went up on the mountain to pray; He continued in prayer for six or nine hours. Do you think it is interesting that this was the same length of time that the disciples were struggling in their trial? We must realize that **if Jesus does not come to us in our trials sooner, it is only because He is still interceding for us before the throne of God!** If "the effectual prayer of a righteous man accomplishes much,"[97] what do you suppose Jesus' prayers accomplish? When He finally comes to us, He will have been sent by the Father as the fulfillment of His own prayers for our care and safety! Hallelujah!

Regardless of what our own hearts say to us in our worst complaining and grumbling, God assures us that no trial will be more than we can endure if we walk by faith in His provisions.[98] **Whether He makes a "way out" or a "way through," one thing is certain: our ability to endure and profit from the trial is due to God's provisions in our lives.** These provisions certainly will be adequate since they come to us from our all-knowing Savior, who has been praying for us during the entirety of our trial. We can be sure that **God's will for us will never take us beyond the place where His grace can sustain us.** This truth comes to us through divine revelation alone; we would never draw this conclusion on our own. That is why the world denies its validity: life seems to contradict it. We must remember that all **truth is uncompromising**; it never yields; it never changes. What you believe will determine the quality of life you will live. Are you living by divine revelation or man's wisdom?

---

[97] James 5:16.
[98] 1 Corinthians 10:13a.

IV

PRINCIPLE FOUR: *God will repeat His tests so that we can learn His lessons from them.*

We ought to remember that this is the second "stormy sea" trial for the disciples. They have been here before; this was truly a deja vu experience. But, being like we are today, they would probably argue that this stormy sea episode was different from the first one, since Jesus was not physically in the boat with them. Without Jesus, they would complain, this trial would naturally be much harder than the previous one.

Is this just an excuse, or would they be giving a sound reason for their failure? I pursue this line of reasoning because so many Christians think this way today. If they do not find an exact and precise example of their own dilemma, they conclude that their situation is a special case, one that is harder and more difficult than that of other Christians.

So we need to ask ourselves, "What was the disciples' first stormy sea trial like?" Jesus was asleep in the back of the boat. He was not rowing with them; He was not bailing water for them; He was not leading them in prayer or in some other way encouraging them to persevere. He was not even acting as a coxswain! The disciples perceived so little action on Jesus' part that they accused Him of "not caring for them."[99] Is this the presence of Jesus that somehow would have made a difference this second time around? I am not inclined to think so. It certainly did not make a difference the first time around.

---

[99] Mark 4:38.

According to Mark 8:17-18, Jesus' presence was only a "memory" away. All the disciples had to do was to RECALL their earlier experience; THINK about what they had heard and seen at that time and then RELATE those recollections to their present circumstances. **There was enough in their past experiences to lead them to trust Jesus to meet their new needs in their present dilemma.** Jesus' physical presence was not necessary. The circumstances did not need to be identical, any more than the circumstances of the feeding of the 5,000 and the feeding of the 4,000 had to be exactly the same before the disciples could apply past spiritual lessons to their new situations.

God repeats His tests so that we can learn our lessons from them. Many times we fail His tests the first time around, right? The Israelites failed to enter the land of Canaan after sending in men to spy out the land and its inhabitants. God had that whole generation, twenty years old and older, die in the wilderness. Then He repeated His trial just east of Jericho beyond the Jordan River. The new generation successfully passed the test, remembering and applying the lessons their parents should have believed.

Jesus asked the disciples to feed over 5,000 people with only five loaves and two fishes. The disciples failed the test. Then He asked them to feed over 4,000 with only "seven loaves and a few small fishes."[100] Unfortunately, they again failed the test. They should have expected the trials to continue to come because God is not concerned about our comfort, but in our conformity to the image of Jesus.[101] Trials are simply the means that God sometimes uses to accomplish this internal transformation process.[102]

---

[100] Matthew 15:34.
[101] Romans 8:29.
[102] James 1:2-4; Romans 5:3-4.

What are the trials that God is repeating in your life? They may be small insignificant ones like having a toilet seat which never seems to be lowered, or bags of trash which never seem to be taken out, or house supplies which never seem to be present, or dishes which never seem to be put in the dish washer (or taken out of the dish washer!), or trying to watch TV with a remote control tyrant.

Other trials may be more trying, like the persistent feeling of being unappreciated, or the perpetual feeling of being worthless, or the constant struggle with finances. And, of course, there are more severe trials than these. Maybe you are dealing with a vast array of emotions stemming from a divorce or sickness in the family or even from the death of a loved one. Maybe you have lost someone in a tragedy like the terrorist strike on the World Trade Center. It came suddenly, and it was devastatingly final.

Whatever your trial is, it seems overwhelming. That is how we feel, and there is nothing directly we can do about that feeling. In addition, maybe your trial does not seem to want to go away. There just does not seem to be any apparent, ready solution to it. And the effect that all this is having on your life? You feel like you are being ground into fine dust; you feel like your very life is being sucked out of you. Desperation sets in, and hopelessness grows more and more intense.

God continues testing the same areas in our lives because He is intent on changing us into the image of His Son, Jesus. **The very persistence of our personal problems is God's way of showing us that life is not in our hands.** We have not been in control; we are not in control; we never will be in control. We may suppose that we have much of our lives "together." But in reality, all of our ability and all of the good fortune we experience spring from the sovereign, gracious, good pleasure of

God.[103] He has allowed our sailing to be as smooth and as successful as it has been. The blessing of a smooth sail is another of God's methods to transform our hearts.[104] Too often we refuse to see God's invisible hand behind the events of our lives. But no one will have a defense when he stands before Jesus and pleads that he had no chance, no reason, no divine instruction, no overture to change.

When we are finally changed by God's divine and gracious intervention, those same trials, which previously were occasions for irritation resulting in a critical, judgmental spirit, become occasions for mercy, resulting in a peace within and a forgiving spirit (if offenders are involved). So, as we take a close look at our lives, we ought to ask this pointed question: "Are we chaffing, or are we being changed into the image of Jesus?" Are we chaffing from worry, or are we being given the peace that passes all understanding?[105] Are we chaffing from feelings of worthlessness, or are we believing that we are God's prized possession?[106] Are we despairing under the feelings of being helpless, abandoned and alone after some great personal tragedy, or are we receiving divine aid each moment from a heavenly Father who cares about us more than anyone else in the whole world?[107] Are we being changed from a person who is hypersensitive to a person who is at rest in the sovereign, good pleasure of God?[108] Our God is a faithful God who *will continue* our trials so that we can learn His lessons from them.[109] If we will learn God's lessons, we put ourselves in the position of having these trials removed. Like a good surgeon, the Great Physician

---

[103] Cf. 1 Corinthians 4:7; 1 Timothy 6:17-19; Romans 2:4.
[104] Romans 2:4.
[105] Philippians 4:6-7.
[106] Ephesians 1:13-14; Tit. 2:11-14.
[107] 1 Peter 5:7.
[108] Cf. Proverbs 12:18; 16:32; 29:20, 22; etc.
[109] Cf. Psalm 119:67, 71, 75.

inflicts pain only to heal and restore. And when the operation has accomplished its desired end, He quickly ends the surgical procedure.

PRINCIPLE FIVE: *Being weary physically and frightened emotionally may hinder our spiritual responsiveness.*

According to the Gospels, the disciples had rowed three or four miles into the teeth of a strong headwind,[110] at night,[111] for six (and possibly nine) hours.[112] Imagine! They had been straining at the oars for at least six hours. That was quite a workout! Remember: they did not want to be in the boat going across the lake in the first place. This was wholly Jesus' idea, and He had to force them to get into the boat.[113]

Jesus does not hesitate to send His followers into the midst of the storms of life; in fact He compels them to enter these trials even against their strongest objections. What He does, we often do not understand at the time.[114] But ultimately, He sends us into trials only to offer an even greater revelation of Himself to us.[115] He is not sending us because He believes we can handle the difficulties. He is sending us in order to reveal to us our weaknesses, our inadequacy to handle the trial, and the need for His strength.[116]

Jesus did not hesitate to send His disciples into a storm that proved to be incredibly difficult. They must have been exhausted after struggling against it so long. Do you think they

---

[110] John 6:19; Matthew 14:24.
[111] Mark 6:48.
[112] Mark 6:47, 48. The "fourth watch" was between 3:00am and 6:00am. Evening in March/April saw the sun set between 7:00pm and 8:00pm.
[113] Matthew 14:22.
[114] Cf. John 11:6-16; 12:16; 13:7.
[115] Matthew 5:4; John 14:21, 23.
[116] Philippians 4:13; cf. 2 Corinthians 12:7-9.

could have entertained less-than-honoring thoughts about Jesus at this point? What do you think they were feeling? They had begun in apathy (We came to this desert place for our own rest and recuperation; we are not really interested in this crowd that has come, and we certainly have no intention of encouraging them to stay longer than absolutely necessary); then, I think, they became frustrated, agitated and touchy when they were compelled to do something they really did not want to do (get into a boat at sunset and begin rowing across the lake). Now they find themselves in a most precarious, if not dangerous, position, being battered by huge waves and pushed backward by an impenetrable wind.

What a pity party they probably had! They even might have gone so far as to blame Jesus for their predicament. They had accused Jesus of not caring for them in their first storm at sea. We should remember also that the disciples were still in a state of hardness of heart as they experienced this new trial.[117] They had not "gotten over" their disappointment of having their personal time with Jesus interrupted by an unspiritual, self-seeking crowd of strangers.[118] The disciples were truly bewildered in addition to being so completely exhausted.

Has your trial led you to have less-than-honoring thoughts about Jesus? Have you blamed God for your situation? Have you accused God of not caring for you? Is the weight of your present trial exacerbated because you have not "gotten over" some previous disappointment or trial? Is life beginning to weigh heavily on you? Is your weary, frightened state proving to be a barrier between you and God? Take heart! Read on! Great news is coming.

---

[117] Mark 6:52.
[118] John 6:14-15, 26-27 seem to allow for this perspective.

It would have been easy to turn around and row to shore with the wind at their backs. Many believers face difficulties this way. When the going gets tough, they do not bail; they bail out! But the disciples did not do this. **They persevered in the strength of their flesh**, heeding Jesus' command to go to the other side of the lake. While some would make perseverance the hallmark of every Christian,[119] it is obvious from this episode that **perseverance can be exerted apart from godliness**.[120] And if it can be manifested apart from godliness, then it cannot be a sure indication of a person's positive spirituality.

When we are out of fellowship with God or just plain carnal, our emotions become tyrants. They destroy the last shred of the residue of happiness and contentment that we previously enjoyed in our walk with our heavenly Father. Fear, anxiety, frustration, anger and bitterness—as well as the dispositions of pride or a critical and unforgiving spirit—can all destroy our peaceful rest in the sovereign goodness of God.

While there is no emotion that is bad in itself, each being a part of God's creative goodness and wisdom, if any emotion leads us away from fellowship with God, then it must be put away immediately.[121] When any emotion or disposition takes us away from the sufficiency of Jesus, we must refuse to follow it; we must not allow it to dictate our responses; we must see such an emotion as sinful; we must confess it, and overcome it by the life that Jesus provides.[122]

As in the disciples case, being weary physically and frightened emotionally may prove to be a great hindrance to our

---

[119] A proposition directly contradicted in 2 Peter 1:6, 9.
[120] This is why the apostle Peter instructs believers to supply "godliness" to their "perseverance" as they journey toward their eternal reward (2 Peter 1:1-11).
[121] E.g., Ephesians 4:31-32.
[122] Cf. Colossianas 3:4, 12-17.

spiritual responsiveness. For this reason, we ought to be ever aware of our physical and emotional state, recalling the fact that:

> "[God] gives strength to the weary,
> And to him who lacks might He increases power.
> Though youths grow weary and tired,
> And vigorous young men stumble badly,
> Yet those who wait for the Lord
> Will gain new strength;
> They will mount up with wings like eagles,
> They will run and not get tired,
> They will walk and not become weary."[123]

Let our self-awareness of our inherent weaknesses lead us to present our "members" (our hands, our feet, our eyes, our ears, our mouths, our minds, etc.) to God for spiritual victory,[124] remembering that His power is perfected in our weakness.[125] **Our weaknesses are not the basis of our failures; our reliance upon our weaknesses is.** Our God can instantly provide His all-sufficient grace, making our weaknesses an irrelevant issue!

---

[123] Isaiah 40:29, 31.
[124] Romans 6:12-13.
[125] 2 Corinthians 12:7-9; cf., 2 Corinthians 4:7ff.

VI

PRINCIPLE SIX: *Because of our sinfulness, we will be frightened even at the solution that God sends for our troubles.*

Jesus came "to them walking on the water."[126] It ought to be one of the surest and plainest inductions of human reason that without the miraculous, man can have no accurate, illuminating account of the life and ministry of Jesus. From His birth to His resurrection and ascension there is no adequate explanation of His life that does not recognize the supernatural. Born of a virgin, cleansing lepers, bringing sight to those blind from birth, strengthening the limbs of the lame from birth, curing every sort of disease and malady, reading the thoughts of man's heart, predicting His own death and resurrection, rising from the dead as predicted, and ascending into heaven before eye-witnesses, and, not to mention, leaving multitudes of transformed lives in the wake of His earthly sojourn, He is at all times conscious of the fact that what He does is directly related to who He is and why He had come. He is the Son of God incarnate, providing a perfect, complete and absolutely free eternal life (salvation) for all who will trust Him for that gift. This life that He gives so freely is the answer to our every real need. Never has there been another like Him. Never has any other claimed to be able to do what He claimed He could do.

Without the miraculous—without God's direct intervention into history—we have nothing to believe *that makes a difference*. The issue is not that we believe something, that we believe some

---

[126] Matthew 14:25.

explanation of the events before us; the issue is that we believe the *right* something—that what we believe is true!

A declaration of Jesus' power and sufficiency

When Jesus came "to them walking on the water," He came to them in a way no ordinary person could come. By coming this way, He wanted to tell them something about who He was and about what He could do (even what He can do *for us*). There are no storms that can hinder Jesus from coming to us. There are no difficulties that He is not Master over. He is above the trial as well as available in the midst of the trial. What is insuperable for us is less than nothing for Him.[127] Is this the Jesus that you have believed in? Is this the Jesus that you are continuing to trust for deliverance in your trials every day? If your Jesus is not supernatural, you have believed in a counterfeit Christ![128]

The water was so turbulent this night and the wind so strong that the disciples could not reach the other side of the lake. Yet Jesus was able to walk upon it! What a contrast this presents: the disciples are straining at the oars, and Jesus is strolling upon the waves. Oh, what a difference THIS JESUS will make in our lives, if we will let Him do so!

Did you notice from the narrative that Jesus did not come all the way up to the disciples in the boat? He came close enough to be seen and recognized, but stopped short of the boat. **It is usual for Jesus to reveal Himself in our lives up to a point, and then to wait for us to respond properly to that manifestation before He comes closer!**[129] Our Lord will use severe trials as the

---

[127] Isaiah 40:15, 17.
[128] Cf. 2 Corinthians 11:3-4.
[129] Cf., John 14:21, 23.

medium through which powerful and comforting manifestations of Himself are given. If we refuse to be motivated by these experiences to worship and trust Him more consistently, He may stop short and come no closer. He does this in order to keep us from being responsible for further light when we are not responding to the light He has given us already. He appears to us in the sunshine to prepare us for His coming in the storms. The time we have to be at ease should be used to prepare ourselves for the storms.[130] If we have experienced His sufficiency in the one, if He has met our needs in the one, how much more will He in the other?

What a miserable, frustrating experience the disciples were having. It was night; the wind, blowing the waves into their boat, produced an invisible barrier between them and their desired destination, the opposite shore. They had rowed three or four miles; they were tired, wet and emotionally drained. At this point we are given an interesting piece of information in Mark's Gospel. He tells us that Jesus had initially "intended to pass them by."[131] If He had passed them by and had left them in their trial, He would have done them no wrong, for He had not promised them a safe or comfortable passage when they began their journey. But, because He is so infinitely good and they find themselves in such a frightful dilemma, Jesus pauses to meet them in their trial by *offering Himself* to them.

Fear unsettles hearts that are spiritually adrift and causes us, as it did the disciples, to mistake the solution to our trial for just another trial. Jesus, walking on the water, was their answer, not another crushing burden to be born. **The distress within their souls resulted from the distrust within their spirit.** When fear controls the heart, the eye of faith finds it difficult to rest

---

[130] Luke 6:46-49.
[131] Mark 6:48.

steadfastly upon its lone, necessary object: Jesus. Have you not found fear to be utterly distracting to your own spiritual walk?

The development of fear

We should observe carefully the sequence of reactions that resulted in the disciples' fearful cry of despair. First, they s*aw* the form coming toward them as it walked on the water. Then, they *evaluated* what they were seeing. Since their hearts were hardened, their evaluation was not related to God or His will. Since they had not "gotten over" their previous disappointment and spiritual failure, their present evaluation was unspiritual; their resulting conclusion was, therefore, distorted.[132]

Then, they became *troubled,* the natural consequence of apprehending a trial in life apart from faith in God and His will. Then, *fear* resulted; it, too, was the natural, emotional response to perceived, impending danger, and since they were without faith, fear had no opponent to vie for control over their hearts. Fear began reigning by default. Then they *screamed* from their fright, showing the connection between our emotions and our speech![133]

Jesus' solution to our fears

If *we* can empathize with the disciples, how much more does Jesus? His empathy led Him to act to relieve their fears. "And immediately," the text says, Jesus spoke to the disciples to allay

---

[132] Cf., 1 Corinthians 2:15—3:3.
[133] Cf., Ephesians 4:29-32.

their fears. And what did He say to allay their fears? Three things: (1) "Take courage!" (2) "It is I." (3) "Do not be afraid!"

What should they do? They should "take courage!" *Why* should they do this? They should do this because the great "I am" is present! No other promise is needed; no other resource is offered! Jesus' presence is more than enough to allay their fears and give them courage. It is everything! And *what* will be the consequence of taking courage at the presence of Jesus, the Eternal and Immutable God who is faithful to all of His promises? They will stop being afraid.

Why is it that most of us refuse to move past our fears unless we are promised that our trial will be of short duration? Why is it that we continue to cling to our past fears unless we are promised that we will not suffer too great a loss in our trial? Why is it that we refuse to let go of our fears unless we are promised that we will ultimately be better off (materially) as a result of our trial? The reason for all of our fears is at bottom one: **we do not trust the goodness and wisdom of God to provide in Jesus all we need for this life.** What we really want is Jesus plus the life we think we should have (or the one we think we need). Is that not true?

Fear of losing all of our material possessions keeps us from accepting God's call to service and intimate fellowship with Jesus.[134] Fear of leaving our friends and family keeps us from accepting God's leading to a ministry that could impact the whole world.[135] **In all of our fears, we distrust God even though we find no sure anchor in anything else in life.**

The disciples were terrified at God's solution for their troubled state. They thought the form upon the water was a ghost instead of God's deliverance. **Failure to recognize and run**

---

[134] Cf. Matthew 19:16ff; Matthew 16:25-26.
[135] Cf. Genesis 12:1-3; Luke 9:57-62.

to the deliverance God supplies leaves us incapable of navigating the storms of life. What we need is an immovable point upon which we can fix our gaze and get our bearing. God knew this, so He sent us His own Son. Jesus is our North Star, fixed and immovable! Find Him; fix your gaze upon Him and He will direct you safely into the harbor of His love. Thomas Aquinas is reputed to have said, "I sought the dove of peace, but it flew away. I looked at Jesus and it flew into my heart." What is true of peace is true of every other virtue as well. Jesus is God's treasury of every resource and blessing imaginable.[136] He is the salve for our eyes, the ointment for our deepest wounds, the brace for our weakened limbs and the pacemaker for our lethargic hearts! When He becomes our life, our weaknesses are swallowed up in His strength.

The only two sources of understanding

Because the disciples would not "get over" their disappointment, they had to rely upon their own perception of their next situation. The Bible calls this walking by sight and not by faith. In each trial that comes our way, we have a choice. We either can respond according to our own impressions, regardless of the source from which we have obtained them, or we can respond according to God's inspired Word. Do not be deceived. There are only two options: (1) God's infallible revelation, and (2) man's fallen reason.[137] Isaiah 55:8-9, one of my favorite passages, records God's declaration of this profound truth:

---

[136] Colossianas 2:3.
[137] Cf. e.g., Job 12:13 and Proverbs 21:30. Romans 11:33-36 says that no man is able to advise God.

> "For My thoughts are not your thoughts, Neither are your ways My ways," declares the Lord. "For as the heavens are higher than the earth, So are My ways higher than your ways, And My thoughts than your thoughts."

Notice that here there are only two options: God's way and man's way. There is *no man* who has God's perspective without obtaining it from God Himself.[138] Since it is *God Himself* who says, "My thoughts are not your thoughts," there can be no appeal of this truth.

Man has not the slightest capacity to have God's perspective on anything, apart from aligning his thoughts with God's finished revelation. As a result, man is incapable of determining which path is the best path to take in life, apart from God's written revelation. These are not unreliable or extreme statements. God Himself states emphatically, "Your ways are not My ways." The very best conclusions that man can form are incapable of bringing him one step closer to God. Man's most reasonable and creative theories all will prove to be empty cisterns incapable of holding any water that might refresh and renew the soul in the time of crisis.[139]

Isaiah's record of God's revelation is a difficult saying only to the one who rejects the depravity of man and the necessity of God's written Word. Such men must be avoided because they will never know God's thoughts or God's ways apart from God's declaration of them in His inspired Word. We must remember that "there is a way which seems right to a man [a way decided upon independently of God's revelation] but the end thereof is death."[140] As a result, every opinion and every piece of advice

---

[138] Cf., Romans 1:21-23, 28; 1 Corinthians 2:9, 14.
[139] Jeremiah 2:13.
[140] Proverbs 14:12.

must first be sifted by the grid of the Word of God before it is received. To fail to do this is to be open to the deception of what, on the surface, appear to be very good ideas. These, however, will never lead to our support and transformation in times of trials, or to our spiritual healing and the continuation of our service for God.

Fear, a great obstacle

The Bible suggests in many different ways that fear is a great deterrent to obedience. You will recall that the angel said to Joseph, when he had decided to release Mary secretly from her betrothal, "Do not be afraid to take Mary [as] your wife." The angel had already appeared to Zachariah, the husband of Elizabeth and future father of John the Baptist, saying, "Do not be afraid . . . your petition has been heard . . ." The angel afterwards appeared to Mary and said, "Do not be afraid . . . for you have found favor with God." And even to the shepherds the angel had to say, "Do not be afraid; for . . . I bring you good news of a great joy . . ."

Taking the terror out of fear

The Bible has much to say about fear. God's declarations about fear are just as inerrant and irrefutable as His declarations about any other topic. While it is always best to discover what the whole Bible says about an issue, there are several lessons about fear in this passage that would be life-changing if we applied them to our lives consistently. First, note that fear is a natural response to certain stimuli that we receive in life. For example, danger, whether it is real or merely perceived, can elicit a response of fear. **The more our evaluations about life coincide with God's, the less we will fear, and the shorter will be the duration of the fear we do experience.** As in the passages given above, after God explains what He is doing, even if He explains it in broad, general principles, man's fears subside. It is easy to see that if anyone is already in possession of God's explanations about life, he has a shield against all manner of fear.

You can remove the fears that you are at this moment experiencing in the crisis that is before you if you seek to obtain and believe God's explanation of your crisis and of those things which are occasioning your fear. Seek a friend who knows the Scriptures well and discover what God has to say about your trial and the response you should give to it. If you will believe God, your fears will subside.[141] A friend of mine did a study on fear while he attended seminary and concluded, "If we will fear God,[142] we will have no reason to fear anything else in life."

Removing the basis for fear

We also learn that fear is meant to alert us, but not to paralyze us. Fear should lead us quickly to trust in God for His deliverance from the danger or trial being perceived. **Fear paralyzes only the hopeless.** As long as any person focuses upon the crisis he is experiencing and has no apparent hope of deliverance, he can be petrified by his fear.[143]

---

[141] John 14:1.
[142] Think of "fearing" God as having a trembling trust in an awesome and majestic Creator. This trust trembles in astonishment at the grandeur that He reveals about Himself.
[143] The fear can be a fear of failure or a fear of harm or a fear of loss or any other fear.

On the other hand, no one is ever paralyzed by fear as long as he perceives the slightest thread of hope. It is not a person's past that is actually devastating to him (regardless of what all the "experts" say); it is whether he perceives any hope in his future. Jesus was raised from the dead to be our constant, living Hope.[144] In Jesus, there is all the hope a person needs to dispel all his fears. Do you know Jesus as your living Hope today?

Removing the perpetuity of fear

Fear is supposed to be a temporary experience. Notice how quickly Jesus attempts to relieve the disciples' fear. This is the case of every single instance of fear recorded in Scripture. **If the fear concerns our safety or well being, God desires to remove it by His own presence, promises and power.** Jesus appears to the disciples in their great distress and says, "Don't be afraid. I'm here now. Don't let your heart be in any further turmoil, for My promises to see you through your trial will be fulfilled.[145] I have demonstrated My power over the wind and the sea before; I will do it again if necessary!"

God wants to handle your fears the same way He handled the disciples fears: He wants to remove them far from you. Just as the sunshine chases away the darkness and shadows, so a living, intimate trust in the Lord will dispel all your fears. "Do not fear, for I am with you; do not anxiously look about you, for I am your God. I will strengthen you, surely I will help you, surely I will uphold you with My righteous right hand."[146] This

---

[144] 1 Peter 1:3-4.
[145] Mark 4:35. Jesus had commanded them to go to "the other side" of the lake, not to go half way and drown!
[146] Isaiah 41:10.

is your inheritance as a child of God and will be your experience as you trust in God's faithfulness to you.

Emotions are powerful. Fear can control you; it can determine how you respond to your situation. As long as you perceive that your life and well being lie in your own hands or in the caprice of life, your fears will determine your responses. Fears can control us because we all understand our own inability to elude the trials and difficulties of life. You know that you are incapable of preventing all the various kinds of trials from coming upon you. Furthermore, **as long as our plans for our lives compete with God's plans for our lives, fear will be our constant companion, whispering haunting premonitions into our ears about ever-present and ever-possible trouble nearby.** But if we hand our lives over completely to God and trust completely in Him, a peace that surpasses all comprehension will guard our hearts and minds.[147]

Removing the tyranny of fear

Lastly, **fear can be controlled**. We should notice that Jesus, the omnipotent and omniscient Son of God commands these disciples to immediately dispel their fears. This instruction comes from their Maker and sustainer, the One who thoroughly knows their capacity, since He knitted together each one of them in the womb stitch by stitch,[148] and the One who had spent the evening praying for them as He watched with care every aspect of their trial. This command comes from the One who knows exactly what is needed to overcome their fears and offers, in Himself, that provision. This direction comes from the

[147] Philippians 4:6-7.
[148] Psalm 139:13-14.

omniscient God who understands the destructive nature of fear and why, therefore, it must be removed as soon as possible. There simply is no way that this is errant advice! If we fail to heed what Jesus says here, we do so to our own detriment, showing the relevance of the truth that **many (all?) of our fears and hurts are self-imposed and self-sustained.**

The fears that you struggle with today can be dealt with right now; not only can they be set aside as undesired tyrants, but also they can be removed from even occasional influences. Jesus who said on the cross that the penalty for your sins has been "paid in full," now says to you, "Take courage. It is I. Do not be afraid any longer." If you can believe Him in the one instance, you can believe in the other. If you can believe Him to deliver you from hell, you can believe Him to deliver you from hellish fears. Will you trust Him to be your Savior from fear as well as your Savior from hell? It is your choice. What's more, it is simple: Jesus is God, and He stands before you now making this promise.

Your only task is to trust Him to do what He promises to do. Look away from your trial and unto Jesus. No one can fix his gaze upon both Jesus and the trial in the same way at the same time. One will always be the grid through which the other will be understood. Which one forms your grid for understanding and living life: Jesus or your problem?

VII

PRINCIPLE SEVEN: *Our present reliance on Jesus always will manifest itself in present obedience.*

What advice would you give to a person who refused to obey Jesus? If someone you know is fearful and distraught like the disciples were, what would you tell him? He refuses to "get over" his past disappointment; he refuses to take courage; he refuses to stop being afraid. What advice would you give him?

Should this person expect Jesus to bless his disobedience? Should he look for God's grace while he refuses to respond as God has asked him to? If he did receive God's grace continually for support while remaining disobedient, would this not be similar to rewarding a disobedient child who refuses to obey? Would not that reward reinforce the child's problem, rather than remove it?

Settling for "relief"

Today, Christians have become content with relief rather than with cure. This is due to the fact that they are being told that they cannot have a cure, at least not immediately. Their problem is so difficult, they are told, that not even the Creator and Sustainer of the universe can cure them. Believing that they are damaged goods, they faithfully follow the latest guru with the latest theory, earnestly longing for even a little improvement, anything that will give them even a glimpse of hope. What a heart-breaking scenario!

Hiding our unbelief

We have become much like the Israelites of old who wanted a king to walk before them. They wanted someone with authority, real or contrived, that they could see and that would fight their battles for them.[149] They wanted to be like the other nations – the pagan peoples – around them. The invisible God, whose unchanging statutes demanded purity and whose ways required faith, needed updating,[150] or so they thought.

The Israelites would have denied that their desires for a king were in any way a rejection of God's rule over them. It would be just fine with them if the king took all his instructions from God. In fact, they hoped this would be true. They would follow God by following the king. Nevertheless, God saw through their charade and authoritatively declared, "They have not [only] rejected you [Samuel], but they have rejected Me from being king over them."[151]

The Israelites probably believed that changes could now evolve by popular vote since the kings would eventually yield to the will of the people. In fact, he was one of them; he would understand them and relate to them. The king could trust God if he wanted to, but they would trust the strength and wisdom of the king. In other words, **they could now walk in the flesh, trusting in the strength and wisdom of man, without it being obvious that they were in rebellion, rejecting God's rule over them.** The king took God's place. And because the king was one step removed from God, to trust him meant relying upon *his* understanding of God's will. How would the Israelites know for

---

[149] 1 Samuel 8:20.
[150] 1 Samuel 8:5. Samuel, and his sons, represent the ways and means of God.
[151] 1 Samuel 8:7.

certain that the king's leadership was a reflection of the will of God to him? There simply was no way.

But how could anyone reproach them? Were they not simply following the man that God would ordain and set before them as their leader? Their king could defeat the oppressing nations, thereby liberating them from the hardships that they were experiencing. But he could not conquer their spiritually rebellious hearts. Once again, the king could give them deliverance from all sorts of oppression, but he could not cure the spiritual problem that kept leading to their oppressions. Consequently, future oppressions were sure to arise as divine chastisements, intended to drive the people back to God.[152]

To obtain the cure to our problems, we must respond in faith to the invisible God who rewards every person who stands upon His will in the face of temptations to do otherwise.[153] The cure is not in us; it is not in the advice given to us by well-meaning people. The cure is in Jesus alone. **His life is our cure!** If I live by His life, a life in which there is no flaw or even the hint of weakness, I can readily experience His divine cure to my spiritual problem whatever it is. Do you know how to experience the life of Jesus Christ? He offers not just a helping hand, He offers His own life for our experience.

Debating Jesus' directions

If you had been in the boat with the disciples, would you have quibbled over Jesus' advice? He said to His despairing and frightened disciples, "Take courage; it is I. Do not be afraid."[154] If

---

[152] Psalm 119:67, 71, 75.
[153] Hebrews 11:6.
[154] A better translation based upon the context might be "Stop being afraid!"

you had been in the boat that night and heard Jesus say these things, would you have replied, "Fine. I will do just that. But *not until* you get into the boat with us, Jesus"? Or maybe you would have said something like this: "No problem. I'll be glad to do this *after* you stop the wind and calm the waves." Or maybe you would have given this response: "Great! *But first* get us to the other side of the lake!"

How often do we reveal the truth about ourselves that **we cannot be happy, that we cannot be encouraged by anyone, that we cannot receive any further truth about ourselves or our present trial UNTIL our situation changes to what we want it to be, and our struggle is gone?** When we act like pouty, little children, is it any wonder that our heavenly Father has to continually discipline us?

I know that there are others who, if they had been in the boat with the disciples and had heard Jesus' advice, would have responded differently. They would have said something like this: "I am *so sorry*, Jesus! Your advice is too simplistic. It will never be that easy."

Such a response brings two thoughts to my mind. First, as I look through our society, I do not find any complicated solutions working! If the simplistic ones are incapable of working, where are the complex ones that are supposed to be so effective? None exist. Second, I am reminded of what the apostle Paul warned the Corinthian church nearly two thousand years ago, when he said, "But I am afraid, lest as the serpent deceived Eve by his craftiness, your minds should be led astray from the simplicity and purity of devotion to Christ." The fact of the matter is simply this: **the power of God is found in the simplicity of Christ!**

Succeeding by following Jesus' directions

Although we find on every hand today people who claim to have better counsel than Jesus, we must not miss the fact that *Peter is transformed by the advice Jesus gives!* I believe that Peter's response should be the norm for every Christian. Every believer can respond like Peter did, stepping away from his victim status and his disobedient lifestyle and living the wonderful life of a victor, if he will simply trust Jesus like Peter did.

Peter would never have gotten out of the boat because of any advice that the other disciples might have given him. And, even if he would have, he would never have had the capacity to walk on the water by that advice alone. Nor would he have found within himself the ability to carry out the advice to walk on water if the other disciples had encouraged him to try it. **Here is what matters: Jesus commanded him to come and with that command He gave him the ability to fully accomplish the command.** What counselor can do this? Do not all counselors simply become to us what the king became to the Israelites? And we still expect God to bless our lives? Amazing!

Mastering temptations, not managing our sinfulness

We must also notice that Jesus does not change the circumstances to let Peter experience less of a trial. The wind did not stop *until after* they got back into the boat. The boat did not get to the other side of the lake *until after* the trial was over. Jesus offered Peter grace to go through the whole trial victoriously. He did not offer to take the trial away. **God's grace transforms even the harshest trial into a sweet experience of the presence and power of God.**

When God removes our trials in answer to our prayers, He must also remove the grace that we could have experienced as well, since it is needed only to go through the trial. If we want to experience more of the grace of God, we must stop demanding that God take away our trials before we begin to respond as He tells us we must. For God to lessen our trial to a "manageable" level is to defeat the purpose for the trial. God sends the trial to make the need of grace more evident and to create a habit of dependence in place of our occasional trust in Him.

Is your life spinning out of control? Control is an illusion for each of us. Only God is able to exercise it! This is the reason that we get so weary of trying to maintain control over our hearts. Such control is simply not within our own power.

VIII

PRINCIPLE EIGHT: *When we respond to God in the midst of our trials, regardless of the severity of our emotional state, we can begin to have immediate spiritual victory.*

At first Peter was paralyzed with fear. Then after Jesus revealed His will in the matter, Peter was confident enough to get out of the boat altogether. Now I want you to consider this seriously for a moment. **Peter was ready to leave behind his last prop against the storm. He was ready to leave behind what little comfort he had left. He was ready to leave behind what little security he thought he had against the raging storm.** Why was he ready to do all this? What brought about this incredible change in Peter? What is the source of his boldness and confidence?

Living in victory by claiming the life

Peter thought Jesus' advice sufficient for him to conquer his trial! Through Jesus' advice, Peter took courage, and stopped being afraid! How was he able to do this? He had recognized Jesus, who alone is the source of all spiritual victory. Such a response to Jesus in the midst of your trial and emotional state takes you beyond yourself. The life you have the opportunity of living—the life you are invited to live—is entirely that of Jesus.

Now understand this carefully: Jesus, who was standing on the water before the disciples, was ready to pass on His life to

Peter so that Peter could do the same thing that Jesus Himself was doing! And what was that? He was standing on the water! Who would try to walk on water by his own ability? Who would be so arrogant, so completely out of his mind, to get out of a boat in the middle of a lake during a killer storm? **There is no self-esteem movement in all the world that is going to make a water walker out of a human being!** There is no counsel that man can give that will secure the same result that the manifestation of Jesus' life within the believer can give. And it is Jesus' life, and nothing less, that God desires in us. Only in His life is the Father well pleased. Only by His life is there victory for us.

Oh, how I wish with all my heart that each reader would grasp the importance of this truth. **Water walkers are God's goal, not copers.** We have far too many Christians trying to cope with life rather than actually walking in spiritual victory throughout their lives. Are you listening to counsel that is trying to advise you on how to "manage" your problems? If you ever get to the point of being able to successfully manage your own problems and the state of your heart, then Jesus died needlessly.[155] As long as we attempt to manage the difficulties in our life, Jesus "will be of no benefit to us."[156] The reason for this is simple: Jesus did not come to give us a helping hand; He came to completely take our place. Just as He was our substitute in dying on the cross, He must become our substitute in living as well.[157] Peter did not need just a little bit of help to walk on the water. Jesus did not say to Peter, "Hey, Peter, do the best you can and I will help out wherever needed." Peter had absolutely no capacity to walk on the water. None! Peter's own life was

---

[155] Galatians 2:21.
[156] Galatians 5:2.
[157] Galatians 2:20.

completely incapable of achieving the task set before him. Peter needed Jesus' capacity to walk on the water, and this capacity was given.

What do you think would happen if Jesus communicated His life to you so you could address your problems with His capacity? Do you think you would continue to struggle so with your fears, anxieties, depressions, loneliness, hurts and weariness? When you read the four Gospel accounts of Jesus, what kind of wisdom, strength, peace, compassion, joy and humility did He manifest? Is He trying to cope with life and its trials or is He ever victorious over them? He is not called "the Lord" for nothing! And He is not supposed to be the Lord of our lives for nothing!

Which approach, coping or constant victory, do you think makes the greatest impression? Which one says the most about God? Which one do you believe is God's revealed will for your life?[158] The kind of life you live will be a reflection of your deepest convictions about these alternatives.[159] It is plain that Jesus offers what no other person can give. Will you continue to judge Jesus and His offer by the advice and weakness of the wisdom of the world?

Describing the life being offered

What is a "water-walking life?" The Scriptures describe for us in symphonic form an incredible, marvelous life that has been won for us, and freely and completely given to us in Christ Jesus. But the life that may be possessed is not automatically expressed. Jesus' life offers the believer the fullness of joy that

---

[158] Cf. Romans 8:35-37; Philippians 4:10-13; 1 Corinthians 10:13; 1 John 3:8; 4:4; etc.
[159] Proverbs 23:7.

comes from walking in the presence of God and communing with Him in intimate fashion. All anxiety, fear and turmoil are cast out and replaced by a peace which passes all understanding, a boldness which rests upon God almighty, and a contentment which is unshaken by the enticements, as well as the trials, of this world. This life is one without weakness or flaw. It takes the believer beyond his own capacities and grants him complete repose in the sovereign good pleasure and providence of God. It hungers and thirsts after righteousness, ruling over all inward lusts and conquering all outward temptations. It is obedient to the revealed will of God in all things. It is dominated by humility and maintains communion with God. It manifests patience, self-control and love in each and every situation in life. It is fullness itself.[160]

Looking to Jesus

As long as you look at yourself and contemplate what you think YOU can do, you will never get out of the boat! Rather, you will drown in your own emotional state as you sit trapped inside the boat, convinced that you must hang on for dear life, since there is no other reasonable response to give. You will continue to be overcome by your trial. You will never move past the experience of strenuously gasping for air as you sink in the turbulent waves of life's storms. When you come back to the surface, the same experience repeats itself over and over again, until you finally have no strength left to avoid inevitable and lasting spiritual defeat. **Only looking to Jesus solves the**

---

[160] Cf. Matthew 5:10, 43-48; Luke 17:3-4; John 15:9-11; 14:1, 27; Acts 3:26; 1 Corinthians 10:13; Philippians 2:2-3, 14; 4:6-7; Colossianas 3:4, 5-11, 12-14; 1Thess. 5:16-18; James 1:2-3; 1 Peter 2:20-22; 1 John 1:7; 3:8; etc.

drowning man's problem! It did so for Peter. And it did so immediately!

How do you "look to Jesus?" You look to Jesus simply by taking Him at His word. If He says, "You're all right," then you are all right. If He says, "Forget your loss," then it is right for you to forget your loss. If He says, "Rejoice," then, regardless of your circumstances, it is right to rejoice. If He says, "Take courage and stop being afraid," then He will provide for you everything you need to be confident and peaceful. Look to Jesus! **Trust Him to give you what He promises and to sustain and care for you by what He gives.**

Discovering what God can do

We are NOT helping people if we do not communicate truth to them when they are sulking and complaining and refusing to be comforted in their distress. They may not want to hear it, so we must communicate it as sensitively as we know how, and with great love and patience. But we MUST communicate it! Truth sets free; error binds.[161] If we allow them to continue in their emotional distress and willful rebellion by not telling them what God requires, then we have reinforced their errant perspective; we have confirmed them in their rebellion; **we have misled them into thinking that God can bless them in their carnal state regardless of how selfishly they are responding.** Disobedience perpetuates spiritual defeat, and spiritual defeat irritates our "hurts."

Peter was able to get out of the boat based solely upon the advice Jesus gave. He did not even seek further encouragement and confirmation from the other disciples. (I doubt that Thomas

---

[161] John 8:31-32; cf. John 17:17.

would have been much help anyway!) **What Peter needed was Jesus' permission and power.** When he received these, he climbed out of the boat. Every other believer can do the same! One thing is certain, however: **No one will ever know what *God* can do if he does not get out of the boat!**

What is it that you need to trust Jesus with today? What is it that is holding you in emotional bondage today? Will you hear Jesus' words and take courage and stop being afraid? Jesus would not tell you to take courage and to stop being afraid if it were impossible to do so. He will give you courage *as* you trust Him; He will set your heart at peace *as* you rest in Him alone. Your trial is His battle.[162] He wants to fight it for you. Will you trust Him to do it?

Analyzing Peter's request

Maybe we should take a moment and consider Peter's unusual request of Jesus. Peter asks Jesus to command him to walk on the water. Now it is obvious that Peter is making this request because he has recognized Jesus and believed Him to be God's Messiah. You do not ask *just anyone* to command you to walk on water! (Can you imagine Peter turning to "doubting Thomas" and asking him to give the command for him to walk on water?) Peter is requesting Jesus to use some of the prerogatives that belong to Him as God's eternal Son and anointed Deliverer.

Is Peter's request a manifestation of *extreme presumption* on his part? What would it prove if Jesus agreed and actually let Peter walk on the water?[163] Would Peter be more spiritual?

---
[162] Cf., Proverbs 21:30-31.
[163] What has it proved in the 2,000 years since it happened?

Would Peter become more responsive and stronger in his faith?[164] Would it prove that Jesus is the Son of God and the Savior of the world? Would Jesus be obligating Himself to always honor such presumptive requests on the part of other believers through the centuries?

Does our familiarity with Jesus lead us to presumptuously ask requests from Him?[165] Does our service for Him lead us to think He owes us something?[166] Do our prayers reveal the presumption that we believe that God is obligated to answer even our sinful, self-centered requests?[167]

Understanding faith

Peter's request was to come[168] to[169] Jesus. Peter did not ask simply to walk on the water. He wanted to walk on the water *all the way* to Jesus. Peter did not want simply to begin walking. He wanted to complete the walk, ending it at Jesus' side. Peter thought he was completely safe in the request he had made. And to Peter's delight, Jesus gave the command that he had sought: *Come!*

At this point, Peter knew the will of God for his immediate life — at least for the next few seconds! He had a direct command to obey. Oh, how wonderful it is when we simply take Jesus at His word! This is faith; nothing more, nothing less. Jesus said, "Come!" Peter obeyed and came; he walked all the way to Jesus.

---

[164] We ought to notice that Peter did NOT think much of this episode after it happened, since he made sure that it was not included in the gospel narrative he helped Mark write!
[165] Cf. Matthew 20:20-28.
[166] Luke 17:7-10.
[167] Hebrews 4:14-16. We must never forget that God's throne is called the throne of "grace." All answers to prayer are due to God's grace toward us.
[168] Probably an egressive (or culminative) aorist is used here.
[169] He wanted to walk all the way to Jesus and be before His face.

By simply responding in faith to Jesus' word, Peter became the only mortal ever to walk on water!

Connecting faith and obedience

Notice how faith is inherent in this obedience? It ought to be inherent in all obedience, but unfortunately it is not. When the obedience appears to us as something we can do by ourselves, we tend to carry it out *without trusting God*. Afterwards we often instinctively sense that our obedience was nothing more than a powerless act of outward conformity.[170]

The reason that we think we can accomplish some things for God is that we do not really understand God's goal in our obedience. His goal is to work on our hearts, not simply to produce outward obedience. Hence, as we obey God, we trust Him to supply what we need for our obedience. Then we must continue to trust God to impact the life of each person with whom we interact as we obey. So, for example, when I love my wife as God directs me in His Word, I must trust Him not only to produce His love for her within me[171] but also to draw her closer to Him by the love that I am giving her.[172] Neither the production of the love nor the drawing of my wife is within my own capability. I must trust God to do both. But I can (and must) manifest God's provision of love in real, tangible ways that are meaningful to my wife. Even in these acts of love, I continue my trust in God for His continued undergirding of my life by His power. As all is *by grace*, all is *in faith* as well.

---

[170] Cf., 2 Timothy 3:5; Matthew 6:1-18.
[171] Galatians 5:22-23.
[172] 1 John 4:9.

Choosing the right role model

As I attempt to set before others the standard found in the Scriptures of a holy, powerful life, I am frequently asked, "How many people do you know who live a life like you are describing? How many really take God at His word and cease from sin?[173] How many manifest the power of God, living victoriously through their trials?" My response is always the same: "That is not the point! The issue is this: 'Has God said it?' If He has, then it is our standard, and it is binding!" There are always enough godly people in every generation to challenge the rest of Christendom to a supernatural life of purity and power, joy and happiness, encouragement and hope. Let's focus on them, making them our model, instead of all the defeated Christians around us.

Can you imagine Moses responding to God in the incredulous way implied above? He would have said something like this, I suspect: "But Lord, how many people are there who lead whole nations out of captivity? I mean, we are talking about hundreds of thousands of people, are we not? And those people have no weapons, right? I mean, such things just are not done today!"

For too long, the Church of Jesus Christ has allowed some within (and some without) its ranks to use man's weaknesses and failures as its standard, instead of God's power and promises. We have become more taken with the obstacles in life than with the omnipotent Sustainer of life. Just listen as the average Christian speaks about the trial facing him. Do his words and attitudes reflect the viewpoint of the ten spies sent

---

[173] I do not teach Perfectionism, i.e., that believers WILL entirely cease from all sin. But it is plainly taught in Scripture that they SHOULD! God's standard will never be perfectly attained in this life (1 John 1:8, 10). Nevertheless, holiness is more than an "ideal;" it is a commandment (1 Peter 1:16-17).

into the land of Canaan to spy out the land, or do they reflect the attitude and words of Caleb and Joshua? No successful company today uses man's failures as the paradigm for its approach to business. Nor do we model our personal lives after failures. We study those who are successful to learn what it takes to become successful. We do not study the failures to decide what can be done and what cannot be done. Why do we use man's failures and weaknesses to determine what is possible in the spiritual realm? May God forgive us!

IX PRINCIPLE NINE: *The same fears and distresses which paralyzed us once will return if we take our eyes off Jesus.*

Peter actually gets out of the boat and walks on water! You have to wonder what it felt like. Was it slippery? Was it shaky? Was it firm? Did he feel mist in his face? Did the hair stand up on the back of his neck or on his arms? This was a thrilling experience! Peter walked all the way to Jesus, just as he had asked to do.

As long as Peter fixed his eyes on Jesus and walked toward Him, he was fine. This is no small statement! He was fine as he walked on the water; he was fine in the midst of the waves and rolling sea; he was fine walking alone without the companionship of his closest friends; he was fine without any visible support against the dangers of his trial; he was fine in the midst of a gale; he was fine emotionally as well as physically; he was fine as long as he looked at Jesus and walked toward Him.

Focusing on your problem is part of the problem

Peter's problem began after he had gone through the difficult part of his trial. After he had arrived at the side of Jesus, he had too much occasion to look again at the obstacles to his faith. As I said earlier, **if you focus on the trial, you will never be able to see the solution!** Your grid for understanding what is before you is all-important. That is why discussing your problems with others can only bring relief but no cure. You may *feel* better after talking about your trial, but you will not *be* any better. Being better comes from talking about Jesus, not by talking about your trial.

Sometimes, it is actually easier, emotionally speaking, to trust Jesus during a great trial. When no other solution presents itself, trusting even in an invisible God is easier. When there is no other option, and the danger is immediate, our trust may feel more like resignation than expectation. Nevertheless, faith is faith, and it will prove to be effective.[174]

Trust must be perpetual

After we have endured a trial by the power of God and for His glory, we sometimes tend to relax spiritually. Pride seeps in, and we begin to think how significant we are to God's plan. We begin to believe that our deliverance was actually related to how we responded in our trial. So, instead of God getting all the glory, we now claim some of it for ourselves.

But, more importantly, we tend to assume that we are now safe because God has just worked in our lives to accomplish a great deliverance for us. **We fail to remember that we are *still standing*, most precariously, *on the water!* How easily and how quickly we are overcome by the next temptation.** We ought to learn from Peter's experience. Jesus wants to encourage us to trust Him as we stand in impossible situations, and He wants to discourage us from thinking that it ever will be the case that trusting Him is optional (that temporarily it is not needed). **Only our continuing trust enables us to continue to stand.** Standing next to Jesus, as Peter was doing, will provide no security for the person whose heart is not continuing to trust in Him!

[174] Mark 9:17-24.

The frailty of miracles

Although Peter had just walked on water, although he was now, after his great feat, standing next to Jesus, when he turned his eyes away from Him and once more focused upon his circumstances, he became frightened all over again. We ought to learn from this that **miracles, in themselves, do not strengthen the heart against temptation. Miracles will not bolster one's faith for long because they are meant to be *signs*, not *foundations*.** Signs point to something else beyond themselves. In fact, every effective sign successfully removes the focus from itself and directs it to another object. There is only one foundation for the life of a person or a church. That foundation, of course, is Jesus Christ Himself.[175]

Connecting faith and thinking

Peter "looked again at the strong wind." He was, in actual point of fact, looking at an obstacle that he had just overcome! Peter ought to have perceived the spiritual significance of his miraculous walk instead of the strength of the mighty wind. But **a presumptuous heart is generally not a pensive heart**. The more God and His providences are contemplated, the less that heart runs wild. Had Peter perceived more of God, his attention would not have been so easily distracted and his emotions so easily troubled once again. As I said earlier, focusing upon your problem is part of the problem!

Jesus' healing of the paralytic is a great example of the main point being made here.[176] The four friends of the paralytic had

---
[175] 1 Corinthians 3:11.
[176] Mark 2:1-12.

either heard about Jesus and His ability to heal or had seen Him actually heal. In addition, they had somehow been divinely impressed that Jesus would heal their friend.[177] As a result, there was no obstacle that they were not willing to confront, no barrier that they were not willing to circumvent, and no sacrifice they were not willing to make to lay their friend before the Great Physician. The better you know Him, the more you trust Him. The more you trust Him the less significant are the trials that lay before you. I wonder how well you know Him today? I mean, I wonder if you *really* know Him?

Life *is* scary! All too often we can find ourselves in terrifying circumstances. A routine day at Columbine High School provides occasion for a couple of students, intent on creating as much evil as they could, to shoot and kill several of their peers and wound others. Oklahoma City experiences the devastation of a tornado that kills and destroys everything in its path. Many face dreaded diseases like cancer and leukemia. Even terrorism is now an ever-present possibility, killing the innocent and creating great fear and uncertainty.

Life may be scary, but Jesus is offering a deliverance which will enable you to do what is otherwise impossible. Is not walking on water impossible? Does not the life described on page 96 seem far beyond your reach? Jesus is offering us a life that would normally be beyond our ability to experience. Every day we have the privilege of giving a response of faith that allows us to experience a life that cannot be explained on a human level. Why would we not want to participate in such a life? Why would we not strive with all of our energy to live it, moment by moment? Why not say with the apostle Paul, "This one thing I do."[178]

---

[177] Cf. the principle found in Psalm 37:4.
[178] Philippians 3:10-14.

The fallacy of worldly wisdom

When we walk toward Jesus, we have to leave behind those who are either so hardened that they cannot respond to Jesus or so entangled with their dilemmas that they cannot focus on Jesus.[179] Most of the wisdom of the world tell us that we cannot get the immediate help Jesus offers here. Most of the advice people give to us tell us that we should not expect to do what other people cannot do. They cannot forgive when they have been wronged, so we should not expect to be able to forgive when we have been wronged. They cannot love again after being taken advantage of, so we should not expect to be able to love again when we have been taken advantage of. They cannot have joy and peace in the midst of trials, so we should not expect to have joy and peace in the midst of our trials. They cannot exercise self-control when they have been severely treated, so we should not expect to exercise self-control when we are severely treated. In the wisdom of the world, another man's failure becomes our limitation. In the wisdom of God, our only limitation is the will of God because His power has already granted us everything for life and godliness.[180]

These counselors of worldly wisdom draw their conclusions about life from their own personal experiences and convictions. Their training will never lead them to a higher standard because they have not been with Christ in the school of faith! Their problem is they have not experienced Jesus! He is offering a life beyond the natural realm, beyond the human capabilities of man, beyond the failures that we all experience. In short, He is offering to let you and me participate in the supernatural. **There is a life being offered that is as different from the natural life**

---

[179] Hebrews 12:1. Cf. 2 Timothy 2:4.
[180] 2 Peter 1:3.

of man as walking on water is different from walking on pavement!** Have you walked on water lately? You want to, do you not? It may look scary, but in reality, **there is no safer place in all the world than upon the water if Jesus is there bidding you to come to Him. Even the boat is not the place to be if Jesus is inviting you to come away from it!**

Peter's miraculous sinking

When Peter took his eyes off Jesus, he experienced the overwhelming fear that he had felt when Jesus was first approaching the boat, before He revealed His identity to the disciples. With his fear came his failure. The text says that Peter "became afraid and [as a result] began to sink."

Now I do not know about you, but I have never seen anyone *begin* to sink! People do not sink gradually; they sink all at once! When the Egyptians followed Moses and the Israelites into the parted Red Sea and the waters returned to their natural place, the texts says that they sank like lead!

Now *that* kind of sinking I am familiar with. When I was twelve years old, my cousin came to visit me. On a hot afternoon we decided to go to the public pool for a swim. He stepped off the deep end of the pool and went straight to the bottom! Only his flailing brought him up again. And when he did come up, he tried to use me for his life raft! His sinking was so quickly that even the lifeguard did not see him go down! There was no cry for help. There was not even an "uh oh!"

I have to wonder how far Peter sank before Jesus' hand lifted him up again. If Peter's sinking was a normal one,[181] Jesus must have known beforehand what was about to happen in order for Him to be able to retrieve Peter when He began to sink. If his sinking was not a normal one, then it is obvious how merciful God is when we stop believing. Oh, how wonderful is the God we worship! His hand of deliverance is ever ready; His power is sufficient; from His love we never can be separated. All that He offers is ours by simple faith.

Peter did not seem to notice the precarious state of his life as long as his water walking went well. This must be one of the reasons God brings trials into our lives, namely, to impress us with our vulnerability. Peter noticed how close to death he was only as he began to sink!

Spiritual deliverance is at hand

Oh, how I wish I could impress each reader who has never placed his faith in Jesus to give him eternal life and to forgive his sins, that he is hanging over the precipice of hell each and every moment. His case is much more desperate than was Peter's. Without Jesus, the unbeliever has no safety net at all. Only the mysterious will of God is sustaining his life until God deems it time to let him go to judgment. Peter's dilemma was unexpected; so will the unbeliever's be! Peter had a saving hand within reach; so it is in the unbeliever's case as well. How close and sure is the rescue that Jesus offers? There is no doubt here; there is no uncertainty. The hand stretched out toward every unbeliever

---

[181] Maybe the Greek text should *not* be pressed to establish a miraculous sinking. But, on the other hand, it should be noticed that Peter did have time to cry out, "Lord, save me," a cry which would take longer to make than a body would need to sink!

may be invisible, but it is no less real. Since it is invisible, it is not up to the unbeliever to find it. It will lay hold of him at the moment he places his faith in Jesus.

The hand stretched out toward each unbeliever is also nail-scarred. Those wounds signify the great love He has for each unbeliever even though He knows every sin that he has ever committed and every one that is still in his future. Knowing all this, He still went to the cross to die for each person. By His death He endured, taking each of our places, the punishment that we deserved. Now by simple faith in Jesus, a person can be pardoned of all his sins and be given, at this instant in time, a new, water-walking kind of life. It is all available for the asking.[182] If you have not trusted Jesus to give you eternal life and pardon your sins, will you do that right now? He will keep His word to you, just as He kept His word to Peter to sustain him as he walked toward Him upon the water.

A different quality of life

The life that Jesus offers is a life that you have never had if you have never believed in Jesus for eternal life. It is a life that is dramatically different from the one with which you are familiar. **Jesus' life *is* spiritual victory.** To the extent that you learn to live by this new life, to that extent you will conquer every spiritual trial that you will ever face! In every single crisis—those you face *before* you get out of the boat, as well as those you will face *after* you get out of the boat—you will be sustained by Him, as He gives to you all you need to triumph in your situation. He dispels fears and gives us courage. He gives the ability to walk on water. He rescues us in all of our failures along the way. But

[182] See John 4:10, 14.

we have to trust in Him like Peter did. You may have to leave your friends, your family, and your co-workers behind. Everyone may think you are foolish, but if you are responding to His invitation to you, all will be well.

PRINCIPLE TEN: *If we do not respond properly to the trial facing us now, we may not be ready for the next trial, which is already on its way toward us.*

Most of the disciples failed this trial because they had failed the previous trial.[1] Failing God gets easier each time it happens. Nevertheless, simple faith, as demonstrated in Peter's response, reestablishes a person's relationship with Jesus so that His power can again be experienced. Philippians 4:13 tells us that God's supernatural power is available to us if we will simply trust Him to grant it. Regardless of the number of spiritual failures you might have had, or how recent they might have been, God's water-walking life is available to you if you only will trust God to give it. Peter chose to turn from self[2] and to begin trusting Jesus once again; the other eleven, as far as we know, remained as they were.

The water-walking life, the walk of faith, is a moment by moment lifestyle. All the disciples[3] at one point had trusted Jesus. But Peter, along with the other ten believing disciples, did not trust Jesus during the feeding of the five thousand. Peter began to trust Jesus again after he recognized Him walking on the water. The others apparently did not begin to trust Jesus again until they were worshipping Him in the boat after the trial was over. Peter, by returning to trust in Jesus, was able to get out of the boat and walk on water. By renewing his trust in Jesus, Peter was able to have an awesome experience that the others

---

[1] Mark 6:52.
[2] "Self" here denotes Peter's own ability, and his evaluation of life, along with the fears resulting from his perception of danger.
[3] Excepting Judas, of course.

could not have because their trust in Jesus had not begun to function again. Unfortunately, Peter stopped trusting Jesus after his own successful water-walking adventure and began to sink. At what point he once again began to trust Jesus is not revealed to us in this episode. But it is clear from all this that walking by faith is a moment by moment affair. **Just because we make one decision to trust God does not mean that our next decision is automatically given in faith.** Living by faith is a necessity for all humans, Christians and non-Christians alike. Living by faith *in God* is a choice that must be made repeatedly, decision by decision, by every believer.

So the issue is always this: **What are you trusting God for right now?** If there is no trust, there is no life flowing from Jesus to you. Without His life, He said, we "can do nothing."[4] Without His life we cannot accomplish His will. **Our ability becomes adequate only by His life!**

After Jesus grabbed Peter and lifted him back up,[5] He rebuked Peter with this statement: "You of little faith, why did you begin to doubt?" Wow! Jesus implies that there was more to experience than what Peter had experienced. If Peter had continued to walk by faith, his experience would have been a constant miracle! As it was, Peter was "up," then he was "down," and then he was back "up" again. This is the same spiritual roller coaster ride that many Christians experience in their everyday lives. They may experience something of the hand of God in their lives in one instance, but in the next, they fail to trust God as they had before, experiencing the frustration and bitterness of spiritual defeat.

---

[4] John 15:5.
[5] Notice that for a very short time Peter stands on the water, as far as we know, without expressing any faith to do so!

We must not pass over the fact that Jesus rebuked Peter's doubt and his lack of faith. Obviously, **a lack of faith, the presence of doubt, and the experience of fear all displease the Lord**. Jesus expects each believer to move from fear to peace, from doubt to faith, and from little faith to persistent faith. As far as God's requirement for each person's life is concerned, spiritual growth is not an option. God expects us to "get over" our past and renew our trust in Him. Not to do so is to imprison ourselves in a jail, keeping the key in our own pocket, and then expecting someone else to open the door for us!

If Jesus stood before you today and asked you the question He asked Peter, what would you say? If He asked, "Why did you in the midst of your trial begin to doubt Me?" what would you say? If He accused you of being a person who did not persist in walking by faith, how would you respond? We can answer these questions now or at the Judgment Seat of Christ. But we will all have to answer them.

Faith made the water walking experience a wonderful reality; fear and doubt turned the experience into a heart-stopping nightmare. We must remember that adversity does not make the man weak or strong; it just reveals what he is already like. It has been said, "Character, like certain herbs and flowers, should give off its finest fragrance when it is crushed." **The trials of life expose the Christian's character and maturity for what they really are.** What is being exposed by your trials? If there are weaknesses, sins and unbelief, will you confess them to God and allow His grace to be sufficient for you today to respond in a completely different manner than you have been responding? Will you amaze the world by trusting Jesus to give you amazing responses to the trials facing you? The resources have already been given, so the choice is yours.

The reason Peter initially passed the trial set before him and the other disciples did not, was not that he had more time to prepare for it, nor that he could see it coming and the others could not. He passed the trial because he responded in faith. Jesus did not invite Peter into a confessional booth before He responded to Peter's renewed act of faith. He did not bludgeon Peter with his failures before He granted Peter water-walking ability. None of these things became a hindrance to Peter's renewed walk.

Jesus will accomplish everything that concerns us. Our job is to fix our eyes back on Jesus and seek to walk in His presence. We trust; He sustains. We commit ourselves to walk toward Jesus in faith; He makes us victorious even in seemingly impossible situations!

Biblical faith always takes the eyes off "self" and places them on Jesus, the lone object of our trust. A person cannot be cuddling his past hurts or abuses or disappointments and walk by faith at the same time. Faith does not look backward at others' offenses or at one's own hurts; it looks forward at God's omni-competence and promised hope. Faith forgets about personal failures and focuses upon God's promised faithfulness.

Every trial is about faith

As we come to the end of our devotional, notice a simple statement in the text: "The wind ceased." As soon as the wind had accomplished God's intended purpose for it, Jesus sent it away. It had come to test THE FAITH of the disciples.[6] This is the purpose of the trial that you are now experiencing as well. If it had been the comfort of the disciples that He had sought, Jesus

---

[6] Cf. James 1:2-3.

could have dismissed the wind while He was still praying on the mountain. If He had not wanted Peter to be tempted twice by its deadly force, He could have dismissed the wind when Peter first got out of the boat and began walking on the water. Jesus is more concerned that we grow up than He is that we have an easy life. If we will grow up—making water-walking our normal experience—life will never be intimidating with trials, or mundane without them!

Connecting faith and worship

Jesus manifested His GLORIOUS PERSON to them by walking on the water, by sustaining Peter as he walked on the water and by quieting the wind and the waves. It was appropriate for the disciples to worship Him because of what they had observed (and experienced!) of His self-disclosure.

I believe that Christians today need to be "stimulated" to praise God by choirs and orchestras, praise teams and dramatic readings, because they have seen so little of God's glory before they come to the Church gathering to begin corporate worship. They have seen so little of His glory because they have lived so little by faith. Grumbling and complaining are always a manifestation of the shallowness of a person's walk with Jesus. I imagine Peter did not have any trouble worshipping Jesus when he got back into the boat! What do you think?

Considering God's methods and goals

In conclusion let me make one last plea by suggesting one last observation to you. **Apart from a study of God's Word and**

a meditation on it, we will never figure out how God works or what His intentions are.

Do you remember the woman that receives physical healing by touching the hem of Jesus' robe?[7] Do you think that allowing someone to be healed that way was a good idea? Could not that approach lead to a very superstitious faith?[8] Surely, such an approach to healing is inappropriate. Surely, such an approach would raise more questions and more objections than are needed or wanted. I can just see it now: Hollywood picks up on this theme and produces a movie about Jesus' clothing. They might even call the movie *The Robe*!

I do not know why God chose to work in this way. But I do know this: if *He* thought it was appropriate, then it *is* appropriate. No Christian has any right to condemn what God allows. We should praise God for it, and adjust our thinking accordingly.

This is true of all of God's ways. No one can tell you why God does all that He does. No one can tell you why He chooses to work with some in one way and with others in another. But what is clear is this: by our diligent study of God's Word we can understand the general principles that will sustain us in every trial we face. Why God does what He does may remain a mystery to us. But how He desires to sustain us and give us comfort, encouragement, and hope should be clearly understood and trusted.

Crisis after crisis is going to come into our lives; this is certain. Job, who was no stranger to trials, says in chapter 5 and verse 7, "Man is born for trouble as the sparks fly upward." Now if you ever have sat in front of a fireplace and watched the heated air take the small sparkling embers up the chimney, then

---

[7] Mark 5:25-34.
[8] Cf. Matthew 9:20 with Matthew 14:36.

you know how naturally trouble comes to us in this life. Later Job says, "Man, who is born of woman, Is short-lived and full of turmoil."[9] So, not only does trouble come naturally to us, none of us is exempted from it.

God never promised a hedge against troubles; He promised a life to handle the troubles when they come. It ought to be obvious that, **if God deems it necessary to provide a supernatural life to deal with crises when they come, every crisis will be devastating if we try to handle it with our normal, human strength and resources.** God's solution will be ours only when God's means are also ours. God's goal is to transform us into water walkers. The means God uses to effect that transformation is appropriating the life of Jesus. Are you going to stay in your boat or are you going to appropriate Jesus' supernatural life to get out of your boat and walk by His power through your trials? That choice is left to you. The difference between drowning and walking on water is the life you choose to live. May God establish you in your trust in Jesus, so that you too can experience a water-walking life!

---

[9] Job 14:1.

About the Author

Dale Taliaferro has been teaching the Bible in churches, on university campuses, in conference rooms, and in homes, both in the United States and overseas, for thirty-seven years. He has been a staff member and director of campus and business ministries, and he has served as a senior pastor. He is the founder of Equipped for Life Ministries (www.e-l-m.org), an organization dedicated to teaching Christians how to live in light of the resources that they have in Jesus. He studied at Western Seminary and Dallas Theological Seminary, and he holds a doctorate in ministry as well as two other degrees in theology and ministry. He and Waunee, his wife of thirty-eight years, reside in Dallas, Texas. They have two grown children.